LEARNING FROM HEBREWS

Charles W. Ford

RadiantBOOKS

Gospel Publishing House/Springfield, Mo. 65802

02-0915

Library of Congress Catalog Card No. 80-67467
ISBN 0-88243-915-4
Printed in the United States of America

A teacher's guide for individual or group study with this book is
available from the Gospel Publishing House (order number
32-0188).

Contents

1
God's Great Son
Read Hebrews 1:1-14

Recently the pastor announced he was preparing a series of Bible lessons on the Book of Hebrews. Many of his people had shown a keen interest in this book. Excitement was running high. Even the youth group decided to join with the adults for the series of Wednesday evening Bible studies. What an interesting sight one could see the first night. Adults and young people entering the church sanctuary carrying not only Bibles but commentaries, notebooks, and other helps.

After an opening prayer the pastor introduced the Bible study with the following statements. "There are many things we don't know about Hebrews. But we won't let this hinder us in our quest for the rich, eternal truths it contains." This is also true of our study. We are not sure who was the human author of Hebrews. Nor do we know the exact date it was written. Through the centuries scholars have debated these issues. Each has given reasons for his beliefs. In our study, too, unanswered questions will not hinder us from gaining eternal truth. Our lives will be spiritually enriched as we invite the Holy Spirit to help us in our search.

God Communicates

God has always sought to communicate with man. Periods of silence were only temporary. When Adam first sinned, God made a way for renewed fellowship. Later when the Israelites sinned, God spoke to them, sometimes in judgment, but always because He cared for them. Hebrews clearly expresses the desire of God to communicate with us. The writer introduces the Epistle with this truth. Notice his words: "In the past God spoke to our forefathers through the prophets at many times and in various ways" (Hebrews 1:1, *New International Version*).

In beautiful language the writer of Hebrews gives us a picture of divine communication. The prophets were the instruments. They conveyed God's message at different times and in different ways. Sometimes the message came as a written law as at Mount Sinai. At other times it was a promise. Or a dream as experienced by Joseph. But God spoke. His message was always clear. Whether it was instruction, history, poetry, or a prophetic utterance, the message was given to meet human needs.

It was not uncommon for men and women in Old Testament times to hear from God. Because they didn't have the complete written Word, God sometimes spoke in an audible voice. How privileged they were to hear God's voice and to receive His message. Even Samuel, when he was a child, received a personal and audible message from God (1 Samuel 3:1-21). What a wonderful experience!

But each of the Old Testament patriarchs and prophets received only a part of the revelation. None of them as individuals received the complete message regarding the Messiah and God's plan of redemption.

God revealed the Messiah's nation to Abraham; Jacob saw the tribe, David the family, and Micah was told the place of birth. These portions of revelation may have seemed fragmentary to Old Testament saints. Indeed they were. Eventually in God's providence they were compiled into a Book we now call the Old Testament. Yet the complete Old Testament was fragmentary and partial even though it was God's full message up to that point in time. It prepared the way for the glorious and complete revelation of God in His Son, Jesus Christ.

God Speaks by His Son

In time past, the writer says, God spoke to our fathers by the prophets, but now He speaks to us by His Son (Hebrews 1:2). Isn't this a beautiful picture of God's eternal love? He communicates to us through His Son, Jesus Christ, our Saviour. It is even more wonderful as we acknowledge that no one merits or deserves it. Not the Jews of Jesus' time nor the Gentiles. None of us do. Yet God takes great pleasure in speaking with us (Revelation 3:20). He freely offers to communicate with any who will hear His voice and respond.

Like the Gospel of John, Hebrews introduces us to Jesus as the Living Word. The writer presents Jesus as the full revelation of the character and nature of God. This is presented in contrast to the Old Testament revelation given through the prophets. In their lives God spoke in various ways, bit by bit, and piecemeal. But the full revelation of God was to come in the person of Jesus Christ. In Him man can see the majesty, power, and nature of God.

Complete redemption, too, is revealed and fulfilled

7

in Jesus. How different from the types and shadows seen in the message of the prophets. They had special beauty and meaning. Each Old Testament type was in itself a jewel containing eternal truth. The splendor of God's revelation in types and shadows is magnified by their fulfillment and complete revelation in Jesus Christ.

In contrasting the Old Testament revelation with the New, Hebrews doesn't suggest any inferiority of revelation. Even though the message to the prophets was fragmentary, each part was fully inspired by the Holy Spirit. Each was God's revelation from that point in time and led to the full and complete revelation of Christ. Other New Testament passages refer to Christ in a similar manner. "For in him dwelleth all the fulness of the Godhead bodily" (Colossians 2:9).

In Hebrews Jesus is portrayed as the highly exalted Son of God. He is appointed by God to be heir of all things and is declared as the one by whom God created the worlds (Hebrews 1:2). With men, inheriting a fortune is a coveted experience. Along with it come prestige and power. But Christ, while possessing great power, refused to use it for selfish purposes. He drank every drop from the cup of suffering and sorrow. Alone in Gethsemane Jesus resisted the temptation for self-deliverance. Little wonder then He was "appointed heir of all things."

But wait—doesn't the Word say we are joint heirs with Christ? Does this mean He will share this inheritance with His redeemed brethren? We answer with a resounding "yes" even though our knowledge of all that it means is limited. To read in Romans 8:17 about our association with Christ as joint heirs should evoke from our hearts a flood of praise and thanksgiving.

8

Brightness of God's Glory

As God's Son, Christ is able to reveal the Father in a way no one else ever could. He is the brightness or visible radiance of God's glory. In Christ we can see this unparalleled glory. But what is it? To what extent can we as finite beings see and comprehend God's glory? We see glimpses of it in some of the Old Testament revelations. Moses did at Sinai. So did Israel on several occasions.

The word "brightness" used in verse 3 is the key to our understanding the exalted position ascribed to the Son. It presents the Son as the Person of the Godhead in whom the glory of that Godhead is manifested. "Glory" denotes the expression of all of the attributes of Deity collectively. To clarify and simplify this we might say: All that God is, including His attributes, is completely and absolutely expressed by Jesus Christ, the Son.

Imagine if you can the impact this glorious truth must have had on the early Hebrew Christians. Those recently converted from Judaism needed to understand and accept Christ as the revelation of God. Jesus had been accepted as their Saviour but He also must be recognized as the brightness of God's glory (Hebrews 1:3)—or the complete and absolute revelation of all that God is. Nothing short of this would do. Then, too, some of the Jews who had been converted for a longer period of time still clung to many traditions. When these traditions conflicted with divine revelation, adjustments needed to be made.

But what about Christians today? Isn't it just as important for us to exalt Christ as God's Son? Shouldn't we too recognize in Christ the expression of all that Deity is? Most certainly. How wonderful it is to bow at

His feet in worship. Or to sing with our lips words of praise and adoration. With the Psalmist our hearts too break forth in praise to our King (Psalm 24:7-10).

God Is in Control

Have you ever wondered how the planets, stars, and other heavenly bodies move in fixed orbits? Or why the distant galaxies don't fall apart, sending individual planets and suns streaking outward in all directions? Although some heavenly bodies seem erratic in their movements, most move in an organized pattern. One can't help but stand in awe when viewing the vast expanse of the universe. But where did this magnificent creation come from? And what is the force that holds it all together? These questions have challenged the minds of men in every generation of time. Reasoning without God, many scientists and philosophers today continue their search for answers.

Yet in clear and simple statements Hebrews gives us the answers. Through inspiration of the Holy Spirit the writer states that God made the worlds by His Son and upholds all things by the word of His power (Hebrews 1:1-3). Christ in His preexistent power and glory was active in the creative process. He was there working in perfect unity with the Father when the worlds were brought into existence. All things in the universe continue to be upheld by the word of His power. God didn't make, then abandon, the creation as some philosophers teach. But rather, He continues to maintain all things through Christ Jesus.

What a marvelous aspect of Christ's work. The display of His power and majesty in the universe is beautiful to behold. It's a faith-building experience for us to view Jesus in relation to His creative and sustaining work. If He cares for the material world, how much greater must be His love and concern for us. If He sees the sparrow fall to the ground (Matthew 10:29), He surely cares about our disappointments and problems. No one who calls on Jesus the Son of God will ever be disappointed.

Christ Purged Our Sins

Up to this point Hebrews stresses the deity of Christ and shows His relationship to the material universe. We have already discussed the glories of His divine nature. Then too we have pictured the wonders of Christ's creative and upholding power. Now as the Holy Spirit guides, the writer deals with another aspect of Christ's work. He moves from describing the cosmic work of the Son of God to show His relationship to human beings. Referring to Christ, the writer declares, He "by himself purged our sins" (Hebrews 1:3). We might paraphrase it by saying He has made purification of sin.

Nothing could take away sin but a perfect sacrifice. Even the Old Testament blood sacrifices and offerings were not designed as a permanent cure for sin. They covered sin until the perfect sacrifice could be made. In due time the Son of God came to earth and was born of a virgin. He lived a sinless life and offered himself in suffering and death to make the atonement for sin. Psalm 22 gives us a prophetic glimpse of the suffering Saviour. In the New Testament Paul tells us, "Christ died for our sins according to the Scriptures" (1 Corinthians 15:3).

As we consider who Christ is and what He has done for us, worshiping and praising Him take on new meaning. Doesn't He deserve our praise? our worship? and our loyalty? Living our lives in obedience to Him becomes our primary goal. In this fleeting pilgrimage of life, true joy and fulfillment only come through serving Jesus.

Yes, the Son of God purged our sins, then "sat down on the right hand of the Majesty on high" (Hebrews 1:3). The cross with all its agony and suffering was behind Him. Atonement for sin was made. Redemption was now complete. His work accomplished, the triumphant Saviour sat down at the right hand of God. Now He would enter the high priestly phase of His ministry.

Better Than the Angels

"Being made so much better than the angels, as he hath by inheritance obtained a more excellent name than they" (Hebrews 1:4). Was Jesus exalted above the angels? Yes. But wasn't He always greater than they? The answer again is yes. Before Jesus took upon himself human form, He was equal with God the Father in every aspect—in power, in glory, and in holiness. But He voluntarily laid aside the independent exercise of some of the divine attributes when He became man. Consequently Jesus prayed to the Heavenly Father for guidance and help (Mark 14:36).

Imagine again the tremendous impact of this truth on the minds of Jewish Christians. Angels held a high position in Jewish thought. Besides being holy messengers, Jesus recognized angels as celestial beings. They were considered mediators of the Law at Sinai. So angels were messengers conveying God's truth to man.

Startling as it may have seemed to some of them, the Jewish Christians needed to accept Jesus as superior to

12

the angelic hosts, far above all in rank and power. Jesus with the Father and Holy Spirit existed eternally. The angels were brought into existence by the creative work of God. None of the angels are omnipotent, nor omniscient, nor omnipresent. But Jesus is. Being equal with the Father He possesses all of the divine attributes.

Finally, Christ as the Son is superior to the angels because of His present position. Here Hebrews quotes Psalm 110:1 in showing Christ sitting at the Father's right hand, a place of highest honor. Soon all enemies will be made His footstool, a symbolic expression of total victory. It is the Father's purpose to establish Christ's kingdom. He will defeat every enemy including death itself (1 Corinthians 15:25, 26).

None of the angels will reign supreme as Jesus Christ will. In contrast, angels are ministering spirits sent forth to serve God for the sake of those who shall be heirs of salvation. Now they surround us to help us (2 Kings 6:17). But our hope for eternal salvation is in Jesus.

2

Our Sovereign Saviour
Read Hebrews 2:1-18

Janet hadn't been saved very long. Reading the Word of God was a joyous experience. Like many new converts she couldn't seem to absorb teaching from the Bible fast enough. After the Wednesday Bible study Janet approached the pastor with a puzzled look on her face. "Pastor" she queried, "I've been reading in the Book of Hebrews and have a question to ask you. In chapter 1, Christ is spoken of as superior to the angels. Then in chapter 2 He is said to have been made a little lower than the angels. Could you explain this to me?"

Perhaps you too in reading this marvelous Book wondered about these seemingly contradictory statements. As we study chapter 2, answers to questions like this will become clear to us. Rather than being problems we shall see them as some of the many glorious, eternal truths revealed in Hebrews.

Don't Drift From the Faith

Often in the Scriptures a single word will convey an important truth. Hebrews 2 is introduced by one of these words. The word *therefore* refers to all that has been said about the glorious person of Christ in the first chapter. His deity, His creative and upholding power, His position high above all creation, His superiority to angels, and His work of redemption are included in this reference.

So, because Jesus is all of this and more we are instructed to "give the more earnest heed to the things which we have heard, lest at any time we should let them slip" (Hebrews 2:1). Several other translations express this verse in another way. Some translate the last phrase "so that we may not drift away from it."

It isn't the gospel that drifts away, but people who hear without giving proper attention drift away from the gospel. We live in environments that often are hostile to the Christian faith. Ungodly forces in the world seek to attract our attention. Satan, the enemy of our souls, doesn't want us to be dedicated followers of Jesus Christ. He will do everything he can to influence a Christian to drift away from all that is good and holy. Usually the temptation comes not as a call to denounce God and reject Christ openly, but just to neglect spiritual responsibilities. To neglect our prayer life, to neglect growing in the knowledge of God's Word and fellowship with other believers can lead to spiritual tragedy. The writer is clear in his warning. "How shall we escape, if we neglect so great salvation?" (Hebrews 2:3).

Since the teaching in Hebrews is directed toward Christians we must take this warning seriously. Failure to give earnest attention to the things of God can result in backsliding and ultimately eternal judgment. Giving priority to selfish interests, increasing desire for worldliness, decreasing interest in spiritual things are symptomatic of neglect. Yes, of neglecting the most precious thing in the universe, the great salvation. But everyone must make his own decision. What is most important to us, Christ or the world? Eternal salvation or eternal damnation?

As a Christian have you ever been troubled about the possibility of drifting away from God? Or the temptations that could lead you away from God? If you have, you're not alone. It's a common experience among Christians. Before you permit yourself to be unduly fearful consider what the Scriptures say. "Greater is he that is in you, than he that is in the world" (1 John 4:4). Victory over the world, the flesh, and the devil belongs to every true follower of Jesus Christ. The risen Christ who lives within us has destroyed the power of sin (Romans 6:6). We will suffer defeat only if we neglect our spiritual responsibilities.

So Great a Salvation

How great are the achievements of man? Consider the wonders of the old world. Babylon's hanging gardens, the gigantic sphinx of Egypt, or the Roman Colosseum are only some of these wonders. We are familiar too with the discoveries and inventions of modern man. Truly God has endowed man with a special genius.

Yet nothing man has ever done can even compare with the great salvation provided by Christ. It is the greatest wonder of the universe. Heaven and earth bow in awe and gratitude for the redeeming work accomplished by the Son of God.

Consider what the writer by the inspiration of the Holy Spirit declares about this wonderful salvation. First he tells us it was spoken of by the Lord (Hebrews 2:3). The words of Jesus are recorded for us in the Gospels. Just what did our Lord say about salvation? Luke 19:10 records, "For the Son of man is come to seek and to save that which was lost." Mark too records the words of Jesus in chapter 10 verse 45: "For even the Son of man came not to be ministered unto, but to minister, and to give his life a ransom for many." Aren't these beautiful words? They reveal, in language all can understand, the ultimate purpose of Christ in coming to earth. From these words we get a glimpse of the infinite love that compelled Jesus to suffer and die on the cross.

Don't you think He deserves our best? our hearts? our lives? And our complete loyalty and dedication to His will?

Hebrews then goes on to declare that the message of salvation was confirmed by those who heard Jesus teach during His earthly ministry. No doubt this would include all who heard and believed the glorious message of salvation proclaimed by Christ. After Pentecost the early believers, endued with power from on high, spread out in all directions carrying the gospel message with them.

Are we faithfully proclaiming that same message of salvation to the lost multitudes of our generation? The apostles are gone, so are the Early Church fathers and the reformers. Today the privilege and the challenge belong to us. Like the disciples we too can call on the Holy Spirit to fill and empower us. Without Him the challenge would be impossible, but with the Spirit's help we can win people of our generation to Christ.

The writer declares yet another fact about this wonderful salvation. Let the Word itself speak. "God also bearing them witness, both with signs and wonders, and with divers miracles, and gifts of the Holy Ghost, according to his own will" (Hebrews 2:4). Time and space will not permit us to describe the mighty works done by the apostles through the power of the Holy

Ghost. Luke records in the Book of Acts many signs and wonders wrought by God through the apostles and other believers. As we read them let's ask God to confirm His Word today in like fashion: Outpouring of the Holy Spirit—Acts 2:1-4; Peter and John—Acts 3:1-10; Apostles—Acts 5:12-16; Philip—Acts 8:26-40; Peter—Acts 9:36-43; Paul and Silas—Acts 16:25-34; Paul—Acts 28:1-6.

But Man Failed

Hebrews emphasizes the supremacy of Christ. In doing so the writer compares the work of angels to the superior ministry of Christ and contrasts man's failure with Christ's victorious work.

Angels have an important ministry in God's kingdom. In the Bible we see them as ministering spirits, yet they will have no authority over the world to come (Hebrews 2:5).

To emphasize God's lofty purpose for man, Hebrews quotes Psalm 8:4-6. This beautiful messianic psalm gives us a glimpse of the role God intended man should play in relation to creation. David expresses a thought that many of us have pondered when he says, "What is man, that thou art mindful of him? or the son of man, that thou visitest him?" (Hebrews 2:6). Still God cares for man. Even though he is a microscopic object in the vast expanse of God's creation, God visits him to love and care for him.

When God created man He made him a little lower than the angels or beneath them in position and rank. But God's purpose was to crown man with glory and honor and set him over creation. So God commanded Adam, the first man, to subdue the earth and have dominion over the animal life (Genesis 1:28).

But man failed. What happened that hindered man from achieving the greatness God purposed for him? SIN. We have all read the Genesis account of man's plunge into sin and the consequences that followed. Although in the intervening years man accomplished great things, sin has kept him from fulfilling God's original purpose. Sin made him fail and caused the God-given scepter to slip from his grasp. Sin is still the destructive force that prohibits man from being the master of creation as God intended. In fact Romans 8:20, 21 indicates that the whole creation is under bondage because of sin. Not until Jesus comes and sets up His kingdom will there be a change.

Our Wonderful Lord

When we view man's failure we cannot help but wonder how God could love us. But He does. Where man utterly failed, God didn't. In Jesus we see the One who fulfilled God's plan that was revealed prophetically in Psalm 8 by David. While incarnate, Jesus was made a little lower than the angels. He truly and completely identified himself with us during His life here on earth, so now He can fully understand our problems—our heartaches, our fears, our weaknesses, and sicknesses. He knows when we are discouraged or disappointed. Jesus understands and cares about our every problem. But He also shares our joys and victories. Little wonder then that our hearts burst forth in praise as we seek to exalt our "wonderful Lord."

Christ is now at the right hand of the Father, crowned with glory and honor. "Wherefore God also hath highly exalted him, and given him a name which is above every name" (Philippians 2:9). Jesus truly is worthy of our praise, of our worship, and of our complete loyalty. His majesty and glory transcend all that is human. Because of our human limitations even our Holy Spirit enlightened minds can comprehend His glory only in part. But some day when we are set free from these human limitations we shall see Him as He is (1 Corinthians 13:12). Until then let's continue to praise and exalt Him with our voices and lives.

Perfect Through Sufferings

Christians the world over are experiencing the joy of serving the risen, victorious Christ. Following Him brings a sense of peace and a feeling of security not found under any other condition of life. Yet let's not forget the joy we find in salvation was not made possible without intense suffering. Our salvation and all the blessings that accompany it were costly. Hundreds of years before Christ came to earth a prophet uttered words describing the sufferings of the Messiah: "Surely he hath borne our griefs, and carried our sorrows: yet we did esteem him stricken, smitten of God, and afflicted. But he was wounded for our transgressions, he was bruised for our iniquities" (Isaiah 53:4, 5).

Still, Jesus didn't suffer for himself. But by God's grace He experienced death for every man. By this He won the victory over death that is a guarantee of our restored dominion over creation. Hebrews says that by His suffering and death, He was made perfect. What does this mean? Perhaps we don't understand all the implications but it does refer to Christ's completeness in the human experience He shared with us. Also He was perfect in the sense of reaching the goal of overcoming all human limitations in our behalf.

20

Because He shared our humanity and voluntarily experienced suffering and death, Hebrews refers to Jesus as the Captain of our salvation. Surely Christ is the founder and leader of our great salvation. No one else can claim this title. Only the One who suffered, and bled, and died on Calvary's cross can lay claim to this title.

Let's not forget as well the great sacrifice made by God the Father. The value He places on a human soul outweighs all other elements of the created universe. His infinite love shines forth brightly from many passages of Scripture. For example, in referring to God the Father Paul the apostle wrote, "He . . . spared not his own Son, but delivered him up for us all" (Romans 8:32). Christ's suffering and death were essential elements of God's eternal plan and purpose. Through it He brought many sons unto glory (Hebrews 2:10). To accomplish this He was willing to let Jesus Christ, His Son, suffer and die on Calvary's cross. This should evoke from our hearts an expression of eternal gratitude. Is love so great in any of us that we would let a child of ours suffer and die for a cause? But God did. May we in solemn gratitude dedicate our lives completely to Him and His purposes.

Not Ashamed to Call Us Brethren

Our Saviour's redeeming work was motivated by infinite love—love that transcends human comprehension. Yet to receive salvation it was necessary that fallen man be cleansed and sanctified or separated unto God. Only then could he worship God in spirit and in truth. Only then could he serve God with a pure heart. How marvelous then—Jesus became our Sanctifier. This was made possible through His blood

21

shed at Calvary, through His Word, and His giving of the Holy Spirit. Jesus accomplished this redemptive work not as one far removed from us, but as a brother. What a mystery! Yet what a privileged position every believer is in. God is not only the Heavenly Father of Jesus but is also the Father of every believer. Even though we often fall far short of God's original purpose for us, Jesus is not ashamed to call us brethren (Hebrews 2:11).

One of the marvels of God's great plan is the fact of Christ's identification with finite human beings. He declares the Father to us and leads in praise to God (Hebrews 2:12). Then too He shares in obedience with us who are God's children and His brothers.

Satan's Power Destroyed

All too often modern man would have us believe the Biblical account of the devil is mythological. He scoffs at the declaration that Satan is an intelligent being. But no amount of criticism or ridicule will change reality. Satan is real. He is eternally opposed to God's plans and purposes. People who yield their lives to his evil powers are courting eternal disaster.

What about believers? Do we need to fear Satan? Does he have any dominion over us? Certainly not. When Jesus died on the cross and rose from the dead He destroyed Satan's power. Satan is the instigator of sin, and sin brings death. It is sin that captivates people, making them subject to eternal death. "The wages of sin is death" (Romans 6:23). But Christ changed it all. By giving us victory over sin He delivered us from the power of Satan and the fear of death (Hebrews 2:14, 15).

Let's accept the freedom and blessing provided by

Christ our great High Priest. If you live under the fear of death, Jesus can deliver you. Trust Him; you won't be disappointed.

He's Always Ready to Help Us

Praise God, we have a merciful and compassionate High Priest—One who understands our every trial and temptation. Because we live in a sinful world, we need help in the hour of temptation. How comforting and reassuring to know that our Saviour is at the right hand of God making intercession for us. Let's learn to trust and lean on Him when temptation seeks to overwhelm us. Christ will not fail us.

3

Christ,
the Faithful Servant
Read Hebrews 3:1-19

Three men responded to a "help wanted" ad for a chauffeur's position. Each was taken by the prospective employer to a cliff. Here they were asked, "How fast could you drive this car and apply the brakes 50 feet before the edge of the cliff and be sure the car would not go over the cliff?"

The first responded, "Forty miles an hour." The second, "Thirty miles an hour." The third answered, "I don't know. I wouldn't take the chance by driving that close to the edge of the cliff to begin with." Which of the three do you suppose got the job?

Unfortunately many Christians today take a similar attitude toward their salvation. "How much of the world can I participate in and still be a Christian?" seems to be a much debated question. Yet most Christians want the inner peace that comes with total commitment to Jesus Christ. Eternal truth revealed in Hebrews 3 will serve as a strong reminder that we shouldn't trifle with our salvation. We shouldn't put God to the test to see how much He will allow. Or how patient He will be with us. Instead, we should follow Christ's example of faithfulness to God.

Consider Our High Priest

Our attention is immediately directed toward Jesus. "Wherefore, holy brethren, partakers of the heavenly calling, consider the Apostle and High Priest of our profession, Christ Jesus" (Hebrews 3:1). This is most important. Why? Because Jesus is the supreme example to follow. As our High Priest, as our Leader, we should follow Him without question. As our Shepherd Leader He will never lead us to the edge of disaster.

In drawing the attention of the readers to Jesus they are addressed as "holy brethren." Holy, not because of who they were by heredity, but because of their relationship to Jesus Christ. They had been cleansed and sanctified by Him; now they are addressed as "holy brethren." Believers today have this same relationship. They too can be called "holy brethren." Having been cleansed from sin we are set apart unto God. We are holy because of the Christ who dwells within us.

Hebrews continues to make another startling revelation. These "holy brethren," the writer states, are partakers of a heavenly calling. A marvelous reference! But what does it mean? How are believers then and now partakers of a heavenly calling? And what is this heavenly calling? This calling is not an invitation to go to heaven, however wonderful and glorious that might be. Although our citizenship is in heaven (Philippians 3:20) this calling refers to the present state of believers who are walking with Christ. Truly it can be called a heavenly state and all who come to Christ are partakers. Although the apostle Paul may not have been describing exactly the same experience, similarities are seen in the following verse: "[God] hath raised us up together, and made us sit together in heavenly places in Christ Jesus" (Ephesians 2:6).

A Faithful High Priest

Faithfulness is an admirable quality. Employers look for it when seeking workers. Businesses and institutions look for this quality in prospective staff members. To achieve any kind of goal, faithfulness to a given task is a must.

Hebrews points to Jesus as the supreme example of faithfulness. In His perfect humanity Jesus was faithful to His Father who made Him His ambassador and our High Priest. It is quite interesting that the faithfulness of Jesus is compared to that of Moses. Although Moses being human did make mistakes, he was faithful to God in all his house (Numbers 12:7). He was a part of God's house or household. Yet unlike many other prophets, he was faithful in all things. He spoke with God and communicated God's message to the people. On several occasions when Israel failed, he stood between them and God's judgment, faithfully interceding for them. Moses then is recognized by God and man as being a faithful steward in all that was entrusted to him.

Still, great as Moses was, his role was that of a servant in God's household. Christ is exalted far above all that Moses was or did. But why? First, Moses was a faithful servant in a system that was temporary. It would fulfill its part in God's plan and then be superseded by an eternal program whose founder and leader is Christ. Second, Christ is not only the One through whom all things were created, He also is the inheritor of all things. So, where Moses was a faithful servant in God's household, Christ the Son of God is the builder and inheritor of this household which includes Moses as well as believers today. Hebrews then exalts Christ far above all that Moses was or did. He is shown as faithful in every way to God's eternal plans.

We then are a part of God's household. When we accepted Christ as our Saviour we were born into God's family (John 3:1-7). What a privilege! God wants us to live as His sons and daughters. He has made abundant provision for our every need. Peace, joy, and love should characterize our lives. When these qualities radiate from us, others will be influenced to take Christ into their lives also.

A Faithful Example

Christ then is God's faithful servant. But isn't He also our example of faithfulness? The One whom we should follow? Of course. Although the Christian church has had many great spiritual leaders, none can compare to Christ. None can take His place as our supreme example. Another apostle pointed to Jesus as the example for believers. "Because Christ also suffered for us, leaving us an example, that ye should follow his steps" (1 Peter 2:21).

As the One whom we should follow, Christ was faithful to God who appointed Him (Hebrews 3:2). What an example of loyalty and faithfulness Christ set for us to follow. Paul the apostle must have caught this vision. His instructions to the Corinthian church clearly demonstrate the importance he placed on following Jesus as the example. "Be ye followers of me, even as I also am of Christ" (1 Corinthians 11:1).

How important is it for us to follow Christ's example of faithfulness to God? Or what benefits do faithful believers receive? Indeed they are too numerous to list and consider individually. Yet one stands out and almost demands our attention. It is something every believer should earnestly covet. We call it VICTORY. Victory over the world, the flesh, and the devil. Victory over selfishness and sin. A victory that causes one to burst forth in songs of praise to God. The basis for this kind of Christian experience is faithfulness to God and His purposes for us.

Wasn't Christ who was faithful to God in all things completely victorious? Didn't He endure temptation without yielding on a single point? Even the grave couldn't hold Him. Faithfulness to God then is the path to living a victorious and productive life—a life that pleases God.

A Solemn Warning

In comparing and contrasting Moses and Christ, Hebrews issues a solemn warning—a warning that no Christian should take lightly. Quoting Psalm 95:7-11 the writer to the Hebrews uses Israel's hardness of heart as an illustration to instruct the Christians.

Before making the application of this Scripture passage, let's look at the historical happening. But first notice how the writer of Hebrews doesn't call attention to the human author of the psalm. Rather he acknowledges the Holy Spirit as the One who is really speaking. Isn't this true of all Scripture? Although God used men as human instruments, He is the one who is speaking. This warning then comes from God.

Israel didn't listen to God although He spoke to them repeatedly through Moses and others. Because of their selfishness and determination to follow their own course the Children of Israel failed God and hardened their hearts. Unbelieving Israel provoked God at Meribah (Exodus 17:7). They had witnessed

God's power in the miraculous deliverance from Egypt. The destruction of Pharaoh's horsemen in the Red Sea surely must have been fresh on their minds. Weren't they also recipients of manna from heaven? Didn't they witness the pillar of fire by night and the cloud by day that led them ever onward? Yet at Meribah they complained bitterly to Moses because they couldn't believe that God would provide water for them.

Unbelieving Israel also provoked God on several other occasions during their 40 years journey in the wilderness. Because of their unbelief, disobedience, and complaining, none of that generation was permitted to enter Canaan. They all died in the wilderness— except Joshua and Caleb.

Hebrews applies the warning given in Psalm 95:7-11 to the followers of Christ. After relating Israel's hardness of heart and consequent judgment, the writer makes the application in these clearly stated words: "Take heed, brethren, lest there be in any of you an evil heart of unbelief, in departing from the living God" (Hebrews 3:12).

We need to guard our lives against the temptations Satan sends our way. They are subtle. "Neglect prayer and fellowship in the Word." "Entertain humanistic philosophies that are prevalent in today's society." "Let secularism dominate your thought life." All of these lead to unbelief and can result in departing from the living God. How tragic. Yet how unnecessary. If we follow the example of Christ as God's faithful Servant we needn't worry about backsliding. As we follow Him daily He will give us spiritual strength to stand against all the subtle temptations of Satan.

Exhort One Another

But what should we do about this warning? Or what responsibility do believers have in keeping their own lives pure and in helping others? Again the Holy Spirit gives us the answer. In verse 13 He encourages us to exhort one another each day while there is still time.

How concerned God is for His people. As a concerned earthly father would, He solemnly warns His children of immediate dangers. Following the warning He gives instructions on how to avoid the spiritual disaster. Although some may view God as a stern Father ready to send judgment, doesn't this verse also reflect His infinite love? Doesn't the father who loves his child warn him of dangers that could destroy him? Our loving Heavenly Father not only warns us of the destructive powers of sin, but also instructs us to help one another.

As Christians living in a decadent society we need one another. Hebrews tells us to exhort one another. Many passages in the Word of God show believers other ways they can help one another to be strong in the faith. Just a few examples are given here to illustrate the kind of relationships God planned for His followers.

1. Love one another (1 John 4:7). Love strengthens any relationship. It is the bond that welds us together in the body of Christ. When an individual Christian senses the love there is for him in the body of believers he is strengthened and encouraged.

2. Pray for one another (James 5:16). Most Christians have experienced the powerful and glorious effects of fervent prayer. Prayer moves the hand of God. It brings crushing defeat to the evil forces that seek to destroy us. Through prayer the children of God are

led from victory to victory. It is not a surprise then that we are instructed to pray one for another. We share and rejoice in helping one another to spiritual victories.

3. Bear one another's burdens (Galatians 6:2). Have you ever carried a burden that seemed too heavy? Or felt defeated because of the heavy burdens you were carrying? Or have you ever desperately reached out to another Christian for help? How understanding and loving our Heavenly Father is to encourage us to share each other's burdens.

Holding Steadfast

These Hebrew Christians, not unlike believers today, constantly faced temptations that could lead them away from God. They encountered many testings and trials. How easy it would have been for them to take the easy way, to slip back into the familiar traditions and customs of their Jewish friends and relatives, or to weave elements of Judaism and Christianity into a new religious pattern. Some did.

But again the warning is clear. "For we are made partakers of Christ, if we hold the beginning of our confidence steadfast unto the end" (Hebrews 3:14). Making a start in following Jesus is most commendable, but a daily steadfastness is also essential. Yet in every generation there were those who made a good start in the Christian faith but lost out for a variety of reasons. Jesus gave us an illustration of this in Matthew 13. In this chapter the Parable of the Sower shows us that some who accept the gospel fail to hold steadfast. For various reasons, such as deceitfulness of riches, cares of the world, neglect of spiritual matters, and persecution, they drift away from the Lord.

We all need faithful warnings, for sin is subtle and deceiving. It often masquerades as a pleasurable and satisfying experience. All around us we see enticements that make sin appear harmless and even beneficial. But sin, if we let it, will weaken our desires to serve God and our trust in His promises. Ultimately it brings eternal judgment and separation from God and all that is pure and good.

Let's Listen and Obey

Hardening one's heart toward God is a most serious matter. The Israelites did, even though Moses gave them strong and courageous leadership. They heard God's voice. It came in many ways. Sometimes Moses spoke the words of God's message. Or it came as a thunderous voice as at Mt. Sinai. Or through Aaron the high priest. Then too God surely spoke to them through the still small voice of their consciences.

One basic principle that's emphasized throughout the Bible is hearing God's voice and obeying. Israel heard but all too often refused to obey. But what happens when people hear and don't obey? First, the unbelieving and disobedient Israelites slowly hardened their hearts. This provoked God to wrath and ultimately to sending judgment.

But what about present-day believers? Is there a danger that we too could hear but not obey? Most definitely. The warning in Hebrews 3:14-19 includes all Christians. In some ways the Hebrew converts faced unusual temptations. Although they had the apostles to teach them God's way, the attraction of Judaism was subtle and enticing. It was always there. The return to the traditions and customs of their forefathers was a powerful temptation. But the warning was clear—hear God's voice and obey.

Believers today must also observe this warning. Our hearts can become hardened and our spiritual desires weakened if we fail to obey God. Many beautiful lives have been marred or even tragically wrecked because this warning wasn't observed.

Still, let's look at the positive side. What a privilege to be able to hear God's voice either through His Word or by the Spirit speaking to our hearts. Think for a moment. God, creator of the universe, loves us enough as individuals to communicate with us. How wonderful to obey Him, to experience the peace and tranquility that results from obedience. Those who listen to God's voice and are quick to act in complete obedience will never have to worry about drifting away. Neither will they harden their hearts or experience God's displeasure and judgment.

4

Christ,
the Giver of Rest
Read Hebrews 4:1-16

They had been traveling all day. The radiant sun shone brightly from a cloudless sky, causing the earth's surface to be heated much beyond the normal. Even though the car had air-conditioning, the driver, along with his family, was uncomfortably warm. As the car rolled along the interstate highway late in the afternoon, everyone seemed unusually tired. Sensing fatigue and tiredness the driver posed a question to his family. "Shall we travel for several more hours?" he inquired. "Or would you like to find lodging soon so we can get an early rest?" It didn't take long for him to get a clear and unmistakable reply. "Let's stop soon," his wife suggested, "we all need rest from the day's traveling."

Have you ever been unusually tired? So tired and weary that all you could think about was rest? Most of us have had this experience. It is common to members of the human family. Our bodies require a certain amount of rest every day.

Although it has a variety of applications, Hebrews has a lot to say about rest. The human author under the guidance of the Holy Spirit uses the word *rest* to convey a most wonderful spiritual truth. This truth is like a diamond that when turned reveals yet another sparkling side.

What Does Rest Mean?

To gain an understanding of this spiritual concept we must look back into chapter 3. Here the writer refers to the complaining Israelites as they provoked God while wandering in the wilderness. Their unbelieving hearts, their disobedience, and their complaining attitude caused God to withhold His choice blessings. Although God longed to bless them, to fellowship with them, and to lead them into the rest of Canaan's land, He couldn't because of their unfaithfulness. Recording God's attitude toward Israel because of their spiritual condition, Hebrews declares, "So I sware in my wrath, they shall not enter into my rest" (Hebrews 3:11).

Canaan then was the *rest* or home that God promised Abraham and his descendents (Genesis 17:1-8). Upon leaving the cruel bondage of Egypt, God didn't intend for Israel to wander 40 years in the wilderness. It was His plan for them to invade, conquer, and possess the Promised Land. Except for Israel's unbelieving hearts, this could have been accomplished only a few months after leaving Egypt. What a glorious *rest* God had planned and prepared for His chosen people! Their omnipotent God was ready to lead them on to total victory. The mountains, sparkling streams, and plains could have brought rest to a weary people. The soil could have produced an abundance of choice foods. But instead of believing God, they tempted and provoked Him. Consequently that generation of adults wasn't allowed to enter the rest God prepared for them.

Believers Are Promised Rest

"Let us therefore fear, lest, a promise being left us of entering into his rest, any of you should seem to come short of it" (Hebrews 4:1). What? Are New Testament believers also promised rest? Has the God of Israel made provision for His people during the church age to enjoy a *rest*? Yes, indeed so. Hebrews gives us a beautiful picture of the rest God has planned for us.

Although New Testament believers are not promised a "physical Canaan," the promise of entering God's *rest* remains open. This promise didn't cease when the Levitical system was fulfilled in Christ. The meaning and promise of *rest* then didn't end when the Israelites entered Canaan. There is in this age a spiritual counterpart of rest that earthly Canaan offered. It is the goal Hebrews encourages every believer to strive for with diligence.

A most interesting fact is that this promised rest is usually referred to as "God's rest." Not only is this true in the Book of Hebrews but also in the Psalms. In Psalm 95:11 God speaks of "my rest" when referring to the promise to Israel. In what sense is it God's rest? Or why is it so designated? Does it simply mean the rest God gives us? Or do we become partakers of something that He himself enjoys?

Genesis 2:2 gives us the first reference to rest in relation to God. It says that on the seventh day He rested from all of His work of creation. This rest has continued and is never said to have been completed. God's rest then has remained open to His people in every generation. It was promised to Israel through the provision of earthly Canaan and is promised to us today through faith in the resurrected Christ. How grateful we should be for this promise. In a world of turmoil, social upheaval, and spiritual apostasy, believers can praise God for His promised rest.

Faith Is the Doorway

Hebrews 4 was the center of a lively discussion. The young adult Sunday school class had been engaged in a study of Hebrews for several weeks. Obviously the interest was high and the students were receiving many new and helpful spiritual insights. Today's lesson focused on the promise of God's rest to Israel and to believers in this age and generation. During the sharing time after the Bible lesson, a pointed question was asked. "I firmly believe this promise," stated a young man who only recently had accepted Christ as Saviour. "But how can a person receive it? Or what does one need to do to enter into the rest God has promised us?"

Wisely the enthusiastic teacher directed the attention of his class to the Word of God to find the answer. "Look at verse 3," he said. "It will help us find the answer. 'For we which have believed do enter into rest.' From this verse it's obvious that FAITH is the key. As is true with all God's promises, faith opens the door that leads to God's promised rest."

Picture a weary soul tired of sin and discouraged with life itself. Carrying a load of sin and guilt is disheartening enough, but add to it the heartbreak it causes in all other areas of life. Broken family relationships, impaired physical health, the terrifying fear of death, and the devastating torment of loneliness are only some. REST. Oh, how a person in this condition longs for rest from his troubles.

If you are one who needs rest, consider the gracious offer of Jesus Christ. "Come unto me, all ye that labor

37

and are heavy laden, and I will give you rest" (Matthew 11:28). Simply believing on the Lord Jesus Christ brings salvation (Acts 16:31). And inherent in this salvation is rest. When we by faith accept the saving message of Christ, we enter the glorious realm of God's promised rest. The guilt, the anguish, the fear of life and death are gone. In their place rises a peace, a contentment, and a completely new outlook on life. Where hate and bitterness once slowly destroyed one's life, now the love of Christ becomes the motivating force. God's rest then becomes the realm into which faith in Christ has brought us. Let us rejoice. Let's invite others to come and join us so they too can share the blessings of this promise.

Unbelief and Disobedience Destroy

Appropriately the Bible not only declares God's promises, it also issues serious warnings. But aren't warnings an indication of God's great love and concern for us? As an earthly father warns his children about dangers, so does our Heavenly Father warn us. He warned Israel, and through His Word God tells us how we can avoid making the same serious mistakes they made.

When God's people fail to benefit from His promises, there is always a reason for it. God is true. His promises are sure. Let the heavens and earth pass away but God's Word will remain (Matthew 24:35). When Israel failed to enter into God's promised earthly rest (Canaan) there was a definite reason—UNBELIEF. But unbelief doesn't stand alone. Disobedience is the outgrowth. Unbelief and disobedience go hand in hand. So, because the Israelites failed to believe God

(Hebrews 4:6, 7) their hearts were hardened and they were not allowed to enter God's rest.

Let's not forget that God is no respecter of persons. If an evil heart of unbelief is found in us will He overlook it? Because we live in the time of grace can we expect God to be more lenient? Or will He judge unbelief and disobedience in a similar manner? Isn't the warning in Hebrews crystal clear? "Let us labor therefore to enter into that rest, lest any man fall after the same example of unbelief" (Hebrews 4:11).

Today is our day. We shall not have another opportunity after this life is over. Let's press eagerly forward to new spiritual heights and depths. Let's strengthen our spiritual lives by seeking the fruit and gifts of the Spirit. Then we can minister to a dying world in the power of the Spirit. Only then can we carry the dynamic message of Christ's love to a world caught in the throes of hopelessness.

Our Sabbath Rest

After a warning about the possibility of missing God's rest, the writer brings us back to the wonders of God's promises (verses 9, 10). In these two verses he likens the believer's promised rest to God's Sabbath rest. What a beautiful picture. We shall see yet another aspect of this most glorious truth.

As we have already observed, a person finds true rest only in Christ Jesus. Prior to receiving forgiveness of sins through faith in Christ, one's life at best is filled with uncertainty. Uncertainty about the present. Or the future. Guilt too plagues the life of a person who is carrying a burden of sin. But, praise God, all this changes instantly when the Saviour is invited to come in. At His command the power of Satan is broken, sins are forgiven, and guilt vanishes. Then we enter into God's most blessed rest. When Christ becomes Lord of our lives, He brings a peace and contentment that was impossible to experience in our former sinful state.

As followers of Jesus Christ we have experienced the joy and contentment of God's rest. No wonder then we can praise and worship God. Praise flows naturally from hearts that have been liberated by Christ. Yet Hebrews tells us of another phase of this rest, one that is an eternal state. There we will not be threatened by conditions that could destroy our relationship with God. Notice carefully what the writer declares: "There remaineth therefore a rest to the people of God" (Hebrews 4:9). The Greek word for "rest" in this verse is *sabbatismos* which means a state of rest, or a ceasing from labor.

This rest is promised to the "people of God" who already have experienced a rest in Christ. It speaks of the eternal rest that every believer longs for. In this present life we are buffeted by evil powers. Temptation constantly challenges our dedication to God. Even though we belong to Christ and are secure in Him, trials and testings confront us. How encouraging, how comforting to know that God has invited us to be partakers of His eternal rest. In that blessed eternal state there will be no heartache. No challenge by satanic powers. No wrestling with worldly and evil forces that seek to upset our faith in Christ.

Diligence Is a Must

But we live in a real world—one filled with evil. On every hand are satanic forces that seek to lure us from our spiritual moorings. The apostle Paul under the guidance of the Holy Spirit described the believer's struggle and clearly identified the enemy. In referring to the wiles of the devil he writes, "For we wrestle not against flesh and blood, but against principalities, against powers, against the rulers of the darkness of this world, against spiritual wickedness in high places" (Ephesians 6:12).

Our adversary the devil (1 Peter 5:8) goes about as a roaring lion seeking to destroy the good, the pure, and the holy. At other times he appears as an angel of light (2 Corinthians 11:14) trying to deceive us. Motivated by this satanic spirit, evil men propagate philosophies that are anti-God. Humanism, secularism, and materialism are taught as supreme guiding philosophies.

The way of the Cross isn't popular. Its demand for complete allegiance and self-denial are too great for many people to accept. Little wonder then that Hebrews 4:11 admonishes the believer to labor (give diligence) to enter into that rest. The warning is most appropriate. Believers today must give diligence so they too don't fall into unbelief as did Israel.

Do we mean that Christians can actually lose out with God? Even after they have received Christ and enjoyed the blessing of salvation? Yes, that's why Hebrews, along with other passages of Scripture, gives such clear and frequent warnings. But how should we respond? Or how can we fortify our spiritual lives so we will not fail to enter God's eternal rest?

First, we should remember that Christ has the power to save us and to keep us. There is no power in the universe that can separate us from Christ (Romans 8:37-39). Evil men, ungodly philosophies, and demonic forces should hold no terror for the child of God. Satan himself flees at the mention of Jesus' name.

Second, we must daily fellowship with God through

prayer and reading His Word. This will strengthen our spiritual lives.

Third, we must live in obedience to His Word. As the Holy Spirit reveals truths from the Bible to us, it is essential that we adjust our lives to this knowledge. Then we will have that blessed assurance: because Christ dwells within, no power can separate us from Him.

The Word Reveals

What would our lives be without God's Holy Word? It reveals His will to us. Unlike the word of man, it is living, active, and authoritative. This living Word fell unheeded on the ears of Israel. They wandered through the wilderness hearing but not believing or obeying. Their rebellious hearts provoked God. Consequently they were not allowed to partake of God's promised rest.

We too have God's Word. It is sharper than any sword, more accurate than any earthly physician's dissecting instrument. It examines our innermost thoughts and lays bare the very depths of our beings. God knows every thought and intent of our hearts. Let's be quick to obey the voice of His Spirit. Let's daily thank God for His Word and its power to guide us in all things.

Our Compassionate High Priest

How comforting to know that when Christ ascended into heaven He began His high priestly ministry. No matter how difficult our situation may be, our great High Priest is interceding for us. He is never indifferent to our needs. Our weaknesses and failings are completely known to Him. He understands our weaknesses and is touched with the feeling of our infirmity. Doesn't the word *feeling* suggest His tenderness toward us? Jesus Christ, our great High Priest, cares.

Having been tempted in all points as we are (verse 15), Jesus is sympathetic with us. He not only understands and cares but also provides help when we need it. We are encouraged to come boldly unto the throne of grace. It is there we obtain mercy and find grace to help in the time of need (verse 16). We have complete assurance that Christ, our great and eternal High Priest will never leave us nor forsake us.

How assuring it is for us to have such a High Priest, knowing that at all times He is not only sympathetic but also stands ready to help. This knowledge should produce a deep-seated feeling of appreciation and gratitude. We are then motivated to respond in praise, worship, and complete obedience.

5

Our Exalted Saviour
Read Hebrews 5:1-14

After reading the Book of Hebrews through several times, a young lady made the following comments. "Isn't Hebrews a wonderful book? Every time I read it," she continued, "new truths seem to spring from the same verses. An outstanding feature that one can't miss is the way the author exalts Christ."

Obviously this young lady had made a most interesting discovery. As we have already learned, Hebrews exalts Christ high above all other beings. Yes, above Moses and Aaron. And even above the angels. The superiority of Christ is emphasized repeatedly. Could this be one reason why Christians are blessed when they read and study the Book of Hebrews? Wherever Christ is exalted and glorified people are blessed.

In chapter 5 the author continues to present Christ as superior. Beginning in tthe last few verses of chapter 4 and on through chapter 5 Christ is presented as the tried and proven eternal High Priest. Aaron ministered in the Old Testament sanctuary, but Christ assumed a totally different kind of high priesthood— one not patterned after the Aaronic priesthood, but one that is eternal.

Characteristics of the High Priest

One thing certain in both Old and New Testament times is that God calls all His people to serve Him. But doesn't the work of God vary considerably? Yes. It follows then that God's people are called to serve Him in many different ways. To serve God effectively in any capacity one needs to develop and cultivate certain traits of character.

Although this is true of all God's servants, it is particularly important for those in places of leadership. The first few verses of Hebrews 5 describe the work of an earthly priest and give some of the characteristics he should possess. After dealing with Christ's high priesthood, the Bible turns our attention to the office of high priest as instituted under the Levitical system. By New Testament times this priesthood had become a political office, the pawn of the Roman government. But this was far from what God had planned and intended. Under the Law the office of high priest was honorable and demanded someone who could act on the behalf of men, someone who could bring their sacrifices for sin and their gifts of tribute to God. What qualities then did a good high priest have? Or what attitudes had to be cultivated if he was to function effectively in his appointed office?

First, he was a man chosen from among men (Hebrews 5:1) so he could act for men in relation to God. Israel needed a mediator to make sacrifices for sin. They were aware of their sinfulness and of the need for sin offerings. The priest also brought the people's gifts to God which would express loyalty to God as the true King.

Second, he could play no favorites. It was essential for him to treat everyone with the respect due to each follower of God. To be sensitive to or touched by the needs and sufferings of others was a must. Compassion for others would help him to serve effectively. Going through the prescribed ritual was in itself not enough. A compassionate heart made the priestly service both meaningful and effective.

Third, he had to be able to bear gently with those who unintentionally did wrong or sinned in ignorance. Or with those who were misled or deceived (Hebrews 5:2).

Fourth, he had to recognize that he himself was clothed with weakness. This weakness often resulted in sin, making it necessary for him to take the humble place along with those he ministered to. Consequently he offered sacrifices for his own sins before he could minister in behalf of others.

A God-appointed Office

Serving God in any capacity should be treated as serious and sacred work. Yet some people take God's work so lightly. Even the Levitical high priesthood had degenerated over the years until it became a symbol of human authority and pride. Traditions and customs evolved until the spiritual emphasis was all but lost.

But this is not what God had originally planned. Listen to what the Word says. "And no man taketh this honor unto himself, but he that is called of God, as was Aaron" (Hebrews 5:4). It was designed to be a sacred office. No one should seek the position because of the prestige and authority it represented. Only those who were specifically called by God could assume the office.

Even Christ did not assume the honor and dignity of the high priestly office on His own (Hebrews 5:4). He, like Aaron, was appointed by God. What an example of humility. Jesus didn't use His power and authority for selfish purposes. In His humility He became the supreme example for us to follow.

But God has called us too. Yes, He has called us in this generation to serve Him. You and I have been appointed by God at this point in time to serve in His kingdom. What a privilege! What a glorious opportunity we have to be workers together with our wonderful Lord. He leads the way. We follow, ever listening to the voice of His Spirit, continually searching His Word, receiving strength and guidance for the tasks He gives us.

Yet in one sense isn't every New Testament believer a priest? Hasn't our God called us to be a holy priesthood? Different, yes, than the Old Testament Levitical system. But notice what the Word says about it when referring to Christ's work on our behalf: "And hath made us kings and priests unto God and his Father; to him be glory and dominion for ever and ever" (Revelation 1:6).

Let us too follow Christ's example of humility. As priests unto God let us pray for the compassion and understanding that is needed to make our service spiritual and effective.

After the Order of Melchizedek

It was not uncommon for some of the early Hebrew Christians to cling to certain parts of the Old Testament system. After all, didn't their religious beliefs originally come from God? For centuries their forefathers worshiped God according to the religious system revealed to Moses and the prophets. Even though they had been converted to Christ, it wasn't easy to suddenly change beliefs—or to leave a system they were trained in as children and was so firmly believed by many friends and relatives.

For several years after Christ's ascension the Hebrew Christians were in transition. Although true followers of Christ, some still practiced circumcision. Others still felt it was a special privilege to be a descendent of Abraham. One purpose of the Book of Hebrews was to help these Jewish Christians to better understand how the old system was completed or fulfilled in Christ. Clinging to the past was no longer acceptable. Now was the time to launch out into the liberty made possible through Christ's atoning work.

Of course the Levitical priesthood was central to the Old Testament system. What would the Law have been without the priests to offer sacrifices and minister before the Lord? Hadn't Aaron and his successors played a prominent role in the religious life of Israel from Moses to the time of Christ?

But Jesus changed it all. To help these Christians understand, Hebrews compares the high priesthood of Aaron to that of Christ. This comparison must have startled some of the Jews. Christ wasn't even a Levite, so how could He be a priest? Hebrews then declares that Christ is a priest, but not after the order of Aaron. His priesthood is after the order of Melchizedek. Quoting Psalm 110:4 Hebrews declares, "Thou art a priest for ever after the order of Melchizedek" (5:6).

Much speculation has been made about Melchizedek. Who was he? Where did he come from? All we know about him is what the Bible tells us. These details will be more fully discussed in chapter 7. For now it is sufficient to say that Melchizedek was a priest of God who prefigured the eternal priesthood of Christ.

Learned Obedience Through Suffering

One of the most difficult things a person needs to learn in life is obedience. From the time we are infants on through adulthood, submitting our will to that of another is a most trying experience. Something within us rebels at obeying someone else. Yet it is one of the most important and necessary disciplines to learn. At times, one's very survival depends on obedience to a law or to someone in authority.

Again Christ is our perfect example. His obedience to all that the Father required was complete and perfect. The Word is crystal clear on this point. "Though he were a Son, yet learned he obedience by the things which he suffered" (Hebrews 5:8). Yes, Christ was obedient. But wasn't He God as well as man? If so, then why was it necessary for Him to submit himself in obedience to anyone? Although with our finite minds we may never understand it completely, the Bible does give us a glimpse into this truth. Doesn't the Word tell us that Jesus was equal with the Father? And though this position in the Godhead was Christ's by virtue of who He was from eternity, He was willing to take upon himself human form. Taking upon himself human likeness, He became a servant and was obedient unto death (Philippians 2:6-8).

In what sense then was Christ obedient? Or to whom did He submit himself in obedience? Wasn't Jesus obedient to His parents? to civil authorities? And didn't He fulfill the Old Testament Law in every detail? Still His obedience in all these areas is demonstrated by His testimony that He came to do His Father's will and not His own (John 5:30). Being human He learned what it means to obey through the sufferings He endured. His obedience to God was perfect.

But why would One so pure, so holy, so powerful submit in obedience to what Christ suffered? There can be but one answer—LOVE. Boundless love, infinite love. Love that extends far beyond human comprehension.

Author of Eternal Salvation

"And being made perfect, he became the author of eternal salvation unto all them that obey him" (Hebrews 5:9). What a marvelous verse. As do many other passages of Scripture, this one declares that Jesus Christ is the source or cause of eternal salvation (Acts 4:12; 16:31; Romans 10:9).

One difficulty some have in understanding this verse is found in the first phrase. How could Christ be made perfect? Was He ever less than perfect? Or was there a progression in His work that brought Him from a lesser level to one that was higher? No, none of these is true. But what then does this phrase mean?

First, this statement doesn't refer to moral perfection. From the beginning Christ was morally perfect—in His preincarnate existence, as a child, in His adulthood—yes, Christ is eternally perfect. There is no place for improvement or development in His moral state. He is perfect.

Second, He was made perfect in the fact that He was tested in every way without ever failing. Wasn't Christ tried under every circumstance, tempted by the devil, betrayed by a friend, and even denied by one whom He loved dearly? Yet He didn't fail. His words as He died on the cross take on new meaning in light of this. When He cried out, "It is finished" (John 19:30), His work was completed. He had met every trial and temptation without failure or sin (Hebrews 4:15). In every instance Christ was perfectly obedient to the will of His Father, even unto suffering and death on the cross. Therefore, He became the author or the source of eternal salvation.

To All Who Obey Him

After beautifully portraying the obedience of Christ, Hebrews turns to emphasize the need for us to follow this example. Having met every test, Christ became the author of eternal salvation *to all who obey Him.*

Although to be saved sinners must obey the teaching of Scripture to confess their sins (1 John 1:9), Hebrews 5:9) is directed more to Christians. It speaks to believers of a continuous flow of eternal salvation.

To clearly understand we need to realize that many Hebrew Christians were at a mental and spiritual standstill. Because they were not moving ahead, they were in danger of falling back into old customs and traditions. Perhaps Christ-rejecting Jews invited them to go back to the temple and depend on the old sacrifices of the Law for favor with God. But they needed to obey God and move ahead, to go on from the rudiments of salvation to the solid meat of the Word. In fact their eternal salvation could be lost if they didn't obey.

What about believers today? Must we too obey God if we are to continue to enjoy the benefits of eternal salvation? Most assuredly. Doesn't Scripture pointedly say that not all who say "Lord, Lord" will enter the Kingdom, but rather those who do God's will (Matthew 7:21)?

But isn't salvation free? Isn't it a gift of God's grace made possible through the meritorious work of Christ? Praise God this is true, or none could ever be saved. Yet the Bible is full of warnings to Christians. These warnings can be summed up in one verse of Scripture. "Examine yourselves, whether ye be in the faith; prove your own selves" (2 Corinthians 13:5).

Spiritual Maturity or Immaturity?

Growing and maturing in spiritual things should be a high-priority item to those who love God. It is imperative that we grow in grace (2 Peter 3:18). Still many Christians are careless about spiritual matters.

Evidently many of the Hebrew believers had failed to grow in the Lord. In fact the writer tells them they are dull of hearing. Or they had failed to gain the spiritual insights so necessary to maturing in their experience. They had been believers long enough now to be teaching others and sharing Christ with them. Instead they needed teaching themselves. Obviously many of the Hebrew Christians hadn't progressed much beyond the first principles of God's Word. They were still in need of milk rather than solid food (Hebrews 5:12).

Yet this wasn't God's will for them and neither is it for believers today. Growth is a must. It pleases God when we are strong in Him. Only then can we withstand the satanic forces allied against us. Only then can we share God's Word with others in a convincing manner.

6

Growing Is a Must
Read Hebrews 6:1-20

Viewing God's creation is a most fascinating and rewarding experience. In the spring flowers blossom, sending their fragrance radiating out into the air around them. Their beauty cannot be matched by anything man with his genius can make. In the countryside one can witness newly born animals and birds following their mothers as they search for life-sustaining food and water. Trees which look almost grotesque without any leaves begin to bud. When this occurs, in a few days leaves will begin to appear until the tree is clothed with a beautiful green foliage.

What does all this mean? And what does it have to do with our studies in Hebrews? GROWTH is the key word. It's one of the laws of nature, a law set into motion by God the Master Creator. It is His design and will that growth in nature takes place.

But isn't growth also a vital principle in the spiritual life of believers? Aren't we admonished and encouraged in many places throughout the Bible to grow and mature in the Lord? Yes, indeed. Our Heavenly Father planned that we should continually grow in the knowledge of His Word and in spiritual stature.

Some of the early Hebrew Christians had failed to

grow and mature in their walk with Christ. We will see crisp and clear warnings along with gentle encouragement to move forward in spiritual things.

Let's Grow in Christ

Salvation is a most glorious experience. Taking that initial step brings a dramatic spiritual change, making one a new creature in Christ Jesus (2 Corinthians 5:17). Sin has been confessed and forgiven, guilt gives way to peace and hope expels despair. Although we were dead in trespasses and sins, at conversion our lives are quickened by Christ, or "made to live" as the original language indicates (Ephesians 2:1).

Yet as dramatic and marvelous as the salvation experience is, God didn't intend it to be a stopping point. Rather, it should be a wonderful beginning of a new life characterized by a continual growing and maturing in the Lord (2 Peter 3:18).

Unfortunately many of the Hebrew Christians had failed to grow. They were like some today who accept Christ as Saviour but fail to grow in the knowledge of God's Word. In the last several verses of chapter 5 the writer mildly rebukes the Hebrew believers for their spiritual immaturity. Notice what he says. "For everyone that useth milk is unskillful in the word of righteousness: for he is a babe" (verse 13).

Guided by the Holy Spirit, the writer to the Hebrews boldly admonishes them. "Let us go on unto perfection" (6:1), he declares. But what is the author saying? Perhaps we could understand his words better if we paraphrased them. "Therefore," he says, "let's go beyond discussing the rudiments of our salvation. Let's stop laying the foundation over again because God has other truths for us to learn and other experiences to help us grow."

Before going on the author lists some of the rudiments or elementary teachings he is referring to. We should remember he isn't minimizing the importance of these truths. What he is saying is don't spin your wheels. Or don't make these rudiments the sum total of your theology. Don't keep emphasizing them again and again while neglecting a whole body of new spiritual truths that God wants you to learn.

Being specific, Hebrews lists six things that fall into the category of foundational teachings.

1. Foundation of repentance from dead works (verse 1)
2. Faith toward God (verse 1)
3. The doctrine of baptism (verse 2)
4. The laying on of hands (verse 2)
5. The resurrection of the dead (verse 2)
6. Eternal judgment (verse 2)

It is very interesting to note that although these doctrines are a vital part of Christian theology they also are represented in Jewish teachings. Each, however, takes on a new meaning within the Christian context. When a converted heathen returned to his former way of life, the change was clearly discernible. But when a Hebrew Christian drifted back toward Judaism, the change was not so noticeable. His beliefs could shift only slightly. The need and importance then of going beyond these rudiments to other distinctive Christian teachings is understandable.

Accepting Christ as High Priest, completely separate from the Aaronic high priesthood, now takes on a new significance. This would take the Hebrew believers beyond their Old Testament teachings, giving them a new picture of the person and ministry of

Christ. This picture can be seen in Old Testament prophecies (Psalm 110:4) but was rejected by most of the non-Christian Jews of that day.

Is there a danger that believers today could fail to grow in the grace and knowledge of God? Or is it possible to drift back into an old way of life, a condition where spiritual things are low in priority rating? Most definitely. We need to use every means God has provided for us. Daily Bible reading, prayer, fellowship with God's people at church, and cultivating an attitude toward life that puts God first will assure one of spiritual growth. Remember, if we are obedient to God's Word in all things, nothing can hinder our spiritual development. Satanic forces, evil men, great trials, or lukewarm Christians cannot negatively affect our walk with Christ if we are obedient.

A Serious Warning

To clearly grasp the seriousness of the warning in Hebrews 6:4-6, we need a broad and deep understanding of the "great salvation." It's free to us—a gift of God. But what did it cost Him? And what price did Jesus, the Son of God, pay for our salvation? Although the full extent of suffering by God the Father and His Son in bringing about redemption is beyond human comprehension, the Word gives us a glimpse into it.

In viewing this great salvation, isn't *love* a key word? As members of the human family we can readily understand human love. In its highest form it is beautiful to behold. Few other forces can motivate one to achieve the highest and noblest deeds. Still great and wonderful as human love is, it has its limitations.

But God's love is infinite. It is limitless and boundless. His love reaches out across the great expanse of the universe to every human being ever born. Speaking of God the Father, one writer declares that He is "not willing that any should perish, but that all should come to repentance" (2 Peter 3:9). Another writer demonstrates God's love for us in these words. "He . . . spared not his own Son, but delivered him up for us all" (Romans 8:32).

Jesus, the Son of God, also demonstrated His love for us by willingly suffering the agony of the Cross. Didn't Christ while hanging on the cross cry out compassionately, "Father, forgive them; for they know not what they do" (Luke 23:34)?

With this background then let's look at the solemn warning given in verses 4-6. For purposes of clarity, let's paraphrase and outline this warning.

It is impossible to renew unto repentance those who fall away if they:

1. Were once enlightened,
2. Have tasted of the heavenly gift,
3. Were made partakers of the Holy Ghost,
4. And have tasted the good word of God and the powers of the world to come,

because they crucify the Son of God afresh and put Him to open shame.

It wouldn't be profitable for us to enter into any of the controversies or varying interpretations of this passage of Scripture. But the warning is clear. To spurn God's love and to treat lightly the redemptive work of Christ on the cross are serious matters. Any Christian who finds himself drifting away from the precious things of God should heed this warning.

Oh, how grateful we should be to God for His goodness in providing eternal salvation. How we should love Him. He deserves our worship, our praise, and our highest loyalty.

Herbs or Thorns and Briars

Simple illustrations using productive or unproductive soil were meaningful to the early New Testament Christians. They depended on the soil for their food. When it failed to produce nutritious grains and vegetables, famine often resulted.

People who are enlightened and have tasted of the heavenly gift and are partakers of the Holy Spirit but who turn their backs on God are compared with unproductive soil. Notice the description of this soil. Like other soil it received regular rainfall. It was cultivated and cared for with anticipation that it would yield a good harvest. Yet it failed to produce a good crop. Much to the dismay of the owner it yielded only thorns and thistles. Needless to say they had no value.

What an indictment against those who know about God's love but willfully crucify Christ afresh. It's like telling God His love isn't appreciated or valued. Or that Christ's atoning death on the cross is less in importance than selfish and temporal desires.

Matthew in the Parable of the Sower gives us a similar illustration (Matthew 13:1-15). The people's hearts are so set on selfish ambitions and so turned off to spiritual things they will never repent. Either God no longer calls them, or if He does they do not hear or respond. On the other hand some soil responds to rain and cultivation and produces an abundant harvest. What a joy to the farmer! How rewarding it must be!

God is pleased too when people respond to His call. What a joy it must bring to His heart when we accept and appreciate His offer of eternal salvation; when we eagerly seek to grow in the knowledge of Christ. Praise and worship flowing from a heart of love must be pleasing to God. Little wonder, then, this person is likened unto fertile soil that with watering and care brings forth an abundant harvest of fruit.

Better Things Expected

Although some of the Hebrew Christians had failed to grow, they were not apostates. They had not turned their backs on Christ. After issuing words of solemn warning the writer hastens to encourage them in the Lord. Notice his words: "But, beloved, we are persuaded better things of you, and things that accompany salvation" (Hebrews 6:9).

But what was there about these Hebrew Christians that motivated the writer to expect good things from them? Or what evidence did he have that they were true believers and sincere in their commitment to God? Although their lives must have demonstrated other evidences of salvation, one verse is unmistakably clear. "For God is not unrighteous to forget your work and labor of love, which ye have showed toward his name, in that ye have ministered to the saints" (Hebrews 6:10).

Isn't love one of the outstanding characteristics of a Christian? They loved God and they loved His people. The divine love that should accompany salvation was abundantly manifested in their lives. How beautiful a picture it must have been to see them minister to the saints in God's name. Keep in mind these were not merely "good works" flowing from a humanitarian spirit. Or a show of religious pride in trying to earn favor with God and man. They gave and ministered because they loved. How encouraging it must have been for them to be reminded that God took notice. He knew their hearts and their motivation.

Still the Holy Spirit through the writer comes back

with more instructions for them to exercise utmost care in their living. Satan would not leave them alone, nor would their Jewish friends stop trying to persuade them to return to Judaism. So the warning came again to this effect: be not slothful (6:12) but rather be diligent (6:11). Take as your examples those who through patience inherit the promises.

Abraham, a Good Example

Abraham surely was a unique individual. He made mistakes and even failed on several occasions. But he possessed a faith in God that surmounted every obstacle. Coupled with this believing faith was a heart willing and ready to obey.

Abraham was not only a giant in faith, but he also exhibited a high degree of patience. He is a marvelous example of both faith and patience. Let's look at several instances from his life. First, he was about 75 years old when God told him to leave Haran. With his natural mind did Abraham know where he was going? No. But he had God's promise. He had God's Word clearly spoken to him.

Second, wasn't he almost 100 years old while still holding faith that God would give him a son? What about Sarah? She was beyond the years for normal child-bearing. The simple fact is Abraham believed God and God fulfilled His promise. Do you think it was easy for Abraham later to take Isaac to Mount Moriah and offer him to God? But Abraham's faith was undaunted. While in the act of obeying he patiently believed that God would meet the need in some way.

Although our faith should be firmly anchored in Christ, what an inspiration Abraham should be to us even as he must have been to the Hebrew believers.

God's Word Is True

One of the many faith-building statements in the Bible is found in this chapter of Hebrews: "It was impossible for God to lie" (Hebrews 6:18). Abraham must have possessed a firm inner conviction that God keeps His promises, that God's Word is absolutely true and reliable. Many of the promises made to Abraham were beyond fulfillment if he trusted in natural circumstances. Didn't God promise to make of him a great nation? And through him all the earth would be blessed? Where was the heir? Or where was the promised son? Wasn't Sarah too old to bear a son? But they had God's promise. They had His Word. Sacred history records the reliability of God's Word and His faithfulness to fulfill His promises.

What a lesson for the early Hebrew Christians to learn. God would not fail them either. His promises to them were just as sure.

Praise God, He is the same today. He doesn't change. What He has promised us in the Word will be fulfilled. In fact, we are encouraged to lay hold on God's promises, to claim them. Let's remember it pleases God to bless and provide for His children.

We Have an Anchor

How encouraging it must have been for these believers to receive God's Word so clearly expressed in this letter. "We have an anchor" (verse 19) proclaims the writer. Christ the great and eternal High Priest was completely aware of their needs. And of ours too. He can sympathize with us in every condition of life. He knows all about our weaknesses and failures, yet He infinitely loves and cares for us.

As our eternal High Priest His work of intercession is effective. He prays for us. By trusting Him, believing Him, and obeying Him, we will grow in spiritual depth. As the Hebrew Christians were exhorted to grow in the likeness of Christ, so are we. This beautiful inspired letter to the Hebrew Christians can also serve as a guide for our lives. The teachings are timeless. If we heed the warnings and obey the instructions given in Hebrews, God will bless us too. Praise God! He is no respecter of persons. We are highly valued by Him.

7

Christ, the Eternal High Priest

Read Hebrews 7:1-28

It was late in the evening, and the men's Bible study class was trying to find a way to bring the interesting discussion to a close. "Isn't the Bible a marvelous book," commented one man. "Our lessons are so interesting and helpful we never want to close." Highlighting the study this night was a discussion of Hebrews 7. But what is so special about this passage? Isn't all the Bible interesting and profitable for reading and study? Of course! Every Book, chapter, verse, and word of the Scriptures was given to benefit us.

Yet focusing on the high priestly ministry of Christ had proven to be a special blessing to the men's group. Their motivation to read and study this chapter was unusual. Interesting discussion questions along with personal application of truth made this class session very special.

A few minutes before the normal closing time a question was asked that sparked a lively discussion. "Who," inquired one of the men, "was this Melchizedek and why was he a type of Christ?" This is precisely the topic we shall focus on in chapter 7.

Although the high priesthood of Jesus is discussed in several places in the Book of Hebrews, chapter 7 presents a detailed historical view. It compares and contrasts the high priesthood of Christ with that of Aaron and Melchizedek. Even though the spotlight seems to be focused on Melchizedek, let's not forget that Christ our eternal High Priest is the central figure.

Melchizedek, Who Is He?

Genesis 14 gives us the circumstances under which Abraham met Melchizedek. Four kings and their armies had invaded the area where Lot, Abraham's nephew, lived. After being victorious in battle they carried away as captives a large number of people including Lot. When the news reached Abraham, he armed his men and enlisted the aid of others and went to the rescue. Near Damascus he overtook them. His attack was successful, the captives were rescued, and the enemy put to flight. Following the victorious venture, on the homeward journey Abraham is met and greeted by Melchizedek.

To many Christians Melchizedek is somewhat of a mystery figure. Outside of Hebrews he is referred to in exactly four verses (Genesis 14:18-20; Psalm 110:4). Most of the information given about him in Hebrews is based on the facts given in Genesis. This illustrious man appears suddenly on the scene of history and then disappears as quickly. It is amazing to many that a man who is proclaimed to be greater even than Abraham was not given a more prominent place in recorded sacred history.

As we introduce Melchizedek, let's ask ourselves a question that many have already asked. Why does Hebrews give such prominence to him when the Old Testament mentions him in only two brief passages? In considering this question, let's remember that a major focus of Hebrews is the *High Priesthood*. Although the high priesthood of Jesus is central to the writer's theme, the Jewish Christian had difficulty understanding it. Being schooled in Levitical teachings, they must have known that every priest had to verify his geneology. To be a priest one had to belong to the tribe of Levi (Deuteronomy 10:8).

When Christ was proclaimed to be their great and eternal High Priest, they may have wondered how it could be. Jesus wasn't a Levite; He was of the tribe of Judah. Let's keep this in focus as we consider some of the facts about Melchizedek, especially as we compare him as a priest to the priestly ministry of Christ.

Let's look at a summary of the facts given in the Bible about Melchizedek.

1. He was king of Salem. Some believe this was the early city of Jerusalem (verse 1).
2. He was a priest of the most high God (verse 1).
3. He met Abraham and blessed him after the successful defeat of the invading kings (verse 1).
4. Abraham honored him by giving him a tithe or a tenth part of what he had (verse 2).
5. He provided bread and wine for Abraham (Genesis 14:18).
6. No record is given of his earthly parentage. His geneology is not given (verse 3).

Honored by Abraham

Without doubt Abraham stands out in history as one of the greats. This is true not only in the Biblical record but also in secular history. Any way we look at Abraham, he was outstanding. Wasn't he an unusual man of God, a pioneer, a traveler, and a successful businessman? Yes, and he also was a skilled warrior when the situation demanded it.

Yet Abraham, the friend of God (2 Chronicles 20:7), manifested a genuine and true humility. He wasn't proud and arrogant. His achievements hadn't affected his view of himself, of others, or of God. Little wonder then that God could use him as a choice servant.

True to his character, the victorious Abraham didn't demand honor from those who came out to greet him after the battle. Even though he had defeated the coalition of kings who had invaded the area, he didn't return expecting a victor's welcome. Instead, Abraham humbly received blessings from Melchizedek and then paid him a tithe. Referring to Melchizedek and the blessings he brought to Abraham, the Scriptures read: "Blessed be Abram of the most high God, possessor of heaven and earth" (Genesis 14:19). The Scriptures also record Abraham's act of showing honor to Melchizedek: "And he gave him tithes of all" (Genesis 14:20). How quickly and beautifully Abraham recognized Melchizedek as one who was superior to him. Hebrews clearly indicates that the one who gives a blessing is recognized as greater than the one who receives it.

Honored Through Abraham

Before considering another highly interesting declaration from Hebrews 7, let's briefly review the role of the Levites in the spiritual life of Israel. Of course, the Levites were descendants of Levi. He was one of the sons of Jacob or Israel. The Levites had a special commission from God. Through Moses He charged them with the care of the sanctuary. When the camp moved, the Levites would transport the tabernacle and its furnishings. When the Israelites were directed to stop traveling, it was the Levites who erected the tent and assisted the priests in their many duties.

Aaron (a Levite) was appointed and anointed high priest. Following this the priesthood was limited by heredity to the descendants of Aaron. Because the priests were of the tribe of Levi, they were also called Levites.

If the priests and Levites ministered, then how were they supported? God made a remarkable provision for them. Through Moses He instructed the Israelites to bring a tithe of their goods which was to support the Levites (Numbers 18:20, 21). In turn the Levites paid a tithe which provided support for the priests (Numbers 18:25-32).

It is at this point that Hebrews makes a most amazing declaration—amazing particularly to the Jewish Christians who had been schooled in the Levitical system. Let's let the Bible speak for itself. "And as I may so say, Levi also, who receiveth tithes, paid tithes in Abraham. For he was yet in the loins of his father, when Melchizedek met him" (Hebrews 7:9, 10). What, did Levi pay a tithe to Melchizedek? Not literally for he was not yet born. But Levi was a great-grandson of Abraham. It was through his ancestor Abraham that Levi honored Melchizedek. In doing so, Levi and Abraham were recognizing the superiority of the Melchizedek priesthood.

Now the Hebrew Christians would be able to understand why the high priestly ministry of Christ was superior to that of Aaron. It didn't follow the Aaronic order of priesthood but was patterned after that of Melchizedek.

Law Cannot Bring Perfection

Now was the time for the Hebrew Christians to thoroughly understand the nature and purpose of the Levitical priesthood. They needed to view it in the right historical perspective. To help them achieve this, Hebrews continues to compare and contrast the high priesthood of Christ with the Levitical priesthood. Unless the Hebrew Christians could once and for all understand and accept the superiority of Christ's priestly ministry, the danger of their drifting back into Judaism was very real.

So Israel, like all humanity, needed a mediator, one who could minister to them and bring them closer to God. To this end God established the Levitical priestly system and gave to Israel the Mosaic Law. Yet as wonderful as the Levitical system was, it had its shortcomings. God didn't intend it to be His final and complete revelation. The author of Hebrews declares with no uncertainty that perfection didn't come by the Levitical priesthood (verse 11) nor through the Law (verse 19). Was this whole system a failure then? Did God make a mistake? Most certainly not. The apostle Paul sums up the real purpose of the Law in Galatians 3:24: "Wherefore the law was our schoolmaster to bring us unto Christ, that we might be justified by faith."

Why then didn't the Law and Old Testament priesthood bring perfection? Or what were its shortcomings? The Mosaic Law didn't provide unfettered access to God. Neither could any be justified through keeping the Law. Being human, the priests were subject to errors of judgment and even willful failure. The Law then was a temporary provision and was not intended to bring perfection. Unfettered access to God and justification by faith would come through a new Per-

68

son and a new high priesthood, one not patterned after Aaron but declared by the Scriptures to be after the order of Melchizedek. This is what the Hebrew Christians must understand and accept. Jesus Christ was their Saviour and eternal High Priest. The perfection not possible under the Levitical system now was available through Jesus Christ. In referring to Christ, the author proclaims, "Thou art a priest for ever after the order of Melchizedek" (verse 17).

Superiority of Christ's Priesthood

Having the complete revelation of God in the Old and New Testaments, we can easily observe the plan of redemption. Our view encompasses the Old Testament types and shadows along with their fulfillment in the New Testament. What a grand and glorious view we have. Our faith is reinforced and strengthened as we daily read the Scriptures. We can readily see and understand how Christ's priesthood is superior to the Levitical priesthood.

Let's try to understand why the early Hebrew Christians had difficulty grasping this precious truth. Remember, they didn't have access to the complete written revelation as we have today. Many probably didn't even have a copy of the Old Testament Scriptures. They were scarce, and few copies were available for the average person to read and study. At least their availability wasn't anything like it is today. Our author, led by the Holy Spirit, leaves no stone unmoved in proclaiming the superiority of Christ's high priesthood. Let's look at some of the facts he presents to convince these Jewish believers.

First, the author declares, "Thou art a priest for ever" (verse 17), indicating the eternal quality of

Christ's priesthood. How different this is from that of Aaron. Every priest under the Levitical system lived his life and in due course died. His scope of service was definitely limited by mortality. What a contrast to that of Christ. Our great High Priest is immortal; therefore He ministers to us through the power of an endless life (verse 16). Christ died once for the sins of all mankind and now having risen from the dead serves eternally as High Priest.

Second, the mediatorial work of Christ makes it possible for us to "draw nigh unto God" (verse 19). Israel under the Levitical system had access to God, but in a limited way. They often came in fear and trembling. Although we too respect and fear God, we are encouraged to come boldly into His presence. "Let us therefore come boldly unto the throne of grace" (Hebrews 4:16). How privileged we are. How blessed we are to have such a High Priest as Christ. Through Him we have free access to God. Moreover it pleases God when we come to Him through Christ. He encourages us to ask largely and make our petitions known (John 15:16).

Third, Christ became "surety of a better covenant" (verse 22). Under the old covenant, priests, who were sinful themselves, offered the blood of animals as atonement for their own sins and the sins of Israel. But look what Christ did. Being the Son of God, He lived a sinless life and died on Calvary's cross for the sins of mankind. With His own blood He made atonement for our sins. But death could not hold Him. Coming forth from the grave and ascending into the heavens, He became our eternal High Priest.

In Bible days surety was a pledge or guarantee often made in money or goods as security for an agreement. Christ our mediator is the surety of the better covenant. He has made himself responsible for all that the new covenant required for our salvation. All the blessings of Grace come to us through Jesus. Let's blend our hearts together in rejoicing. Christ, the eternal Son of God, is our guarantee. Having conquered every evil force, even death and the grave, He alone could guarantee our salvation.

Fourth, the author declares that Christ's priesthood is unchangeable (verse 24). How different this was from the Levitical system. Although God gave Moses specific instructions to regulate the functions of the priests, being human they often failed. Their ministry sometimes was rendered ineffective because of their weaknesses. Then, too, each priest served until death. None could complete the work he started. But again let's look at Christ. His priesthood is eternal and unchangeable. How reassuring it is to know this. The compassionate, understanding, and intercessory ministry of Christ will not change (Hebrews 13:8).

Saves to the Uttermost

In many ways the Levitical priests were powerless. They could serve in the temple and make offerings, but they couldn't save anyone. Even serving with the highest motivation, the priests were limited in what they could do for the people. How different is the high priestly function of Christ. A verse that has blessed the hearts of millions tells the whole story. "Wherefore he is able also to save them to the uttermost that come unto God by him, seeing he ever liveth to make intercession for them" (Hebrews 7:25). How marvelous! How wonderful! The eternal Son of God is able to save us completely. But what does this mean?

First, no one is so deeply mired in sin that Jesus can't

reach him. Christ will save anyone who earnestly desires to be saved and humbly repents. God's mercy and love are as vast as the universe. Second, Christ can save us eternally. We are persuaded, as was the apostle Paul, that nothing can separate us from the love of God in Christ Jesus (Romans 8:37-39). We are saved to the uttermost. Christ will keep us as long as we are determined to love and serve Him. Remember, He lives forever to make intercession for us.

Our Perfect High Priest

What a glorious note on which to end this chapter. Christ is declared to be the perfect High Priest. He is not subject to change, to error, or to favoritism. Aaron and many of his successors served admirably and faithfully but they were human and subject to all that being human implies. Christ is perfect because of who He is. This perfection is reflected in His high priestly ministry. It is eternally fitted to meet the needs of His people. As we look at the high priestly ministry of Jesus our faith should rise to new levels.

8

A Better Covenant
Read Hebrews 8:1-13

Accepting Christ as central to God's plan of salvation is a must for all who would become born-again believers. Heresies and false teachings about the person of Christ have risen periodically in history. Some religions totally reject Christ as the Son of God and the Saviour. Yet a distorted view of the person and work of Christ can be just as devastating. Both can result in a dependence on something or someone other than Christ for eternal salvation. Hebrews was written to lead the Jewish Christians into a clear understanding of who Christ is and of His work in God's plan of redemption.

Having established the superiority of Christ as the eternal High Priest, the author goes on to deal with other related themes. There were still many other truths these believers needed to know and accept. This was essential if they were to grow into mature Christians—necessary too because some were in danger of drifting into a form of religion that was a mixture of Old Testament rituals and Christian teachings.

We Have Such a High Priest   *TODAY!*

Referring to all that has been taught about the

priestly ministry of Christ, the writer to the Hebrews declares, "We have such a high priest" (verse 1). What a marvelous teacher the Holy Spirit is! Knowing all things, He dealt in detail with the specific doctrinal weakness and needs of these believers. In the first seven chapters the Holy Spirit, through the writer, led the Hebrew Christians step by step through a most difficult and sensitive subject. Systematically the Spirit dealt with the questions and problems that arose as they considered the relationship between Christ and the Old Testament Levitical priesthood. Christ has been presented as superior to Moses, Aaron, the prophets, and the entire Levitical system. It included not only the priesthood but the sacrificial system with all its offerings.

Let's remember some of this teaching may have been difficult for some of the Hebrew Christians to accept and follow. After all, the author is asking the Hebrew Christians to commit themselves to a most difficult task. Laying aside some of the beliefs taught them in childhood wasn't easy. Didn't their forefathers have an illustrious history? Wasn't it they who received through Moses the revelation of the Law? Now they are being asked to lay aside some of these beliefs and to acknowledge and accept someone who is greater.

But praise God we have such a High Priest! One who is eternal and unchangeable. One who knows what it means to be tempted and can sympathize with us. One who even though He was God took upon himself human form, manifesting eternal love by suffering the cruel death on the cross.

Seated at God's Right Hand

After His resurrection from the dead and when His

74

earthly ministry was completed, Christ returned to heaven. Hebrews tells us He is seated at the right hand of God. The apostle Paul too, writing about the exaltation of Christ, declares, "He raised him from the dead, and set him at his own right hand in the heavenly places" (Ephesians 1:20).

What a beautiful picture. Christ, the crucified and risen Saviour, sitting at the right hand of the Majesty on high. Not only was His redemptive work completed, but it was also accepted by God. All that He did while on earth was pleasing to God: the conduct of His life and ministry and His suffering and death were done in complete obedience to God. In Ephesians Paul declares that being seated at God's right hand, Christ is "far above all principality, and power, and might, and dominion" (1:21). Our faith should rise to new heights as we see Him in this exalted position. (when praying)

A Minister of the Sanctuary

Being seated at the right hand of God doesn't mean that Jesus is inactive. Even though His atoning work was completed to perfection, He would now enter another phase of ministry, the high priesthood. In describing this for us the author calls Christ "a minister of the sanctuary, and of the true tabernacle, which the Lord pitched, and not man" (Hebrews 8:2).

Notice the progression of teaching, the step-by-step approach used by the Holy Spirit. After Christ is presented as the eternal High Priest, He is now shown as ministering in the heavenly tabernacle. How marvelous! How glorious! Being our High Priest, Christ is ministering there at the throne of God in our behalf. In Hebrews 7:25 the writer declares that He ever lives to make intercession for us. Yes, Christ prays for you and me. He did while He was engaged in earthly ministry (John 17:9), and He continues to intercede for us today.

When we are discouraged, or tempted, or fearful, let us be assured that our High Priest is praying for us. We must never forget that no matter what happens here on earth, no matter how hopeless our circumstances may seem, Jesus is there in heaven interceding for us. We can come to Him and receive the grace and strength needed to do God's will and to find spiritual victory. Let us also remember that when our cup overflows and all things are going well, Jesus is still there ready to present our praise and worship to the Father. And to share our joy.

Comprehending and understanding the scope of Jesus' ministry of intercession is greatly important for every Christian. Doesn't it make possible every other spiritual ministry on earth? Isn't it Jesus himself who calls and appoints men for ministries in the Church (Ephesians 4:11, 12)? It follows, too, that the Church as the body of Christ is edified and built up by what each member receives from Christ and gives out to others (Ephesians 4:16). We greatly appreciate this kind of ministry. But we are aware that it could not be effective if it were not for our great High Priest who is interceding continually for us there at the Throne.

It was highly important then for the Hebrew Christians to see Jesus in a true perspective. But what about us today? Isn't it just as important for us to see Jesus as the eternal High Priest? Unfortunately, some think of Jesus as a babe in a manger. Others think of Him hanging on the cross. Of course both are true, He did experience the manger and the cross. But His earthly ministry prepared Him to enter the glorious high priestly ministry which is now going on.

So, Christ is now ministering in the heavenly sanctuary. But the earthly sanctuary must have been very real to the Hebrew Christians. Many of them still went to the temple at the regular hours of prayer (Acts 3:1). Even the disciples were proud of its splendor and beauty (Matthew 24:1). Its priests with their beautiful robes were a very impressive sight. To many, this may have seemed far more real than something in heaven.

Yet in a short time the earthly temple would be destroyed and its ministries would then come to an end. This could be a terrible shock to the Hebrew believers if they weren't prepared for it. Understanding the high priestly ministry of Christ would help. Knowing that He ministers in the true heavenly sanctuary as their High Priest would prepare them for what was to come. NEED TO MAKE IT (HIM) REAL!

Shadow of Heavenly Things

Startling as it may have been to the Hebrew believers, they are told that the Levitical priests and their ministry in the temple were types or shadows of what was to come. The Law with its system of sacrifices was not permanent. Aaron and his successors, though appointed by God, were limited in scope and time. Their work too was temporary. It all foreshadowed a new and glorious way, one in which Christ would become the eternal High Priest.

Does this mean that the Levitical system—including the earthly tabernacle and ministering priests—wasn't important? Or that it was of lesser value? No. Everything God ordains or institutes is of immeasurable value. Even though the tabernacle and priestly

77

functions were designed by God to be temporary, they were important to the Israelites because it was their means of fellowship with God and of providing a cover for their sins.

Referring to the priestly functions under the Levitical system, the writer states that they "serve unto the example and shadow of heavenly things" (verse 5). What does the writer of Hebrews mean by this verse? If we paraphrased his statement it would read, "The earthly priests minister in a sanctuary that is a copy and shadow of the heavenly one."

Typology is a rich and rewarding study. Although some scholars have gone beyond the bounds warranted by sound Bible interpretation, we shouldn't hesitate to seek the rich truth found in types and antitypes. As the Hebrew Christians came to realize the tabernacle and priestly system were copies of the heavenly reality, how could they turn back? They needed to understand how the Levitical system played an important part in Old Testament times but now had been superseded by something better, something glorious and eternal.

Mediator of a Better Covenant

Hebrews uses several important words. To properly understand the text we should know their meanings. Let's look at two of them.

1. *Mediator.* In New Testament times a mediator was one who negotiated for both parties and brought them both to the same goal. Thus Jesus as Mediator brings God to us and brings us to God.

2. *Covenant.* A covenant is a solemn binding agreement or a declaration of purpose.

Now we are told that since Christ's ministry in

heaven is more real and more excellent than the earthly symbols, it must be built on a better covenant. This better covenant would be established on better promises. Moses was mediator of the old covenant under the Law. But his ministry, though great, only foreshadowed the better ministry of Christ as He now mediates or guarantees the conditions of the new covenant. Consider what the Holy Spirit says about this through the mind and pen of the author of Hebrews: "But now hath he obtained a more excellent ministry, by how much also he is the mediator of a better covenant, which was established upon better promises" (Hebrews 8:6).

Better is a word often used in Hebrews and sometimes misunderstood by students of the Bible. Why is one of God's creations or programs better than another? Or why would God establish a covenant relationship with man and later replace it with one that is better? To answer these and similar questions we simply say, that's the way God designed it. Perhaps sinful mankind wasn't ready to receive God's best before Christ came. As Paul wrote, the Law was a schoolmaster to bring us to Christ (Galatians 3:24). At God's appointed time Jesus made His entrance into human history. Even though He came unto His own and they received Him not (John 1:11), a new and glorious day had dawned for the world.

The Babe who was born in Bethlehem's manger was ordained by God to become the Saviour of all who would believe on Him. He would die a cruel death on Calvary's cross but rise triumphantly from the grave. Upon ascending into the heavens, Christ became our eternal High Priest. Now He lives to make intercession for us. Indeed a new day had dawned. A new covenant was made. Now because of God's grace, sinful man can come for cleansing from sin. He can be filled with the Holy Spirit and come boldly to God in prayer. Praise God we have a better covenant.

A New Covenant Promised

Have you ever made a promise or agreement with God and then failed to keep it? Perhaps you made a promise to pray more consistently or to witness as opportunities arose. Then slowly you drifted back into the same condition as before the promise. Israel failed, too, in their covenant relationship with God.

After leaving Egypt and during the 40 years in the wilderness they broke the covenant God had made with them. But God is merciful and compassionate. Although He couldn't condone Israel's sins and waywardness, He promised to make a new and better covenant with His people. Hebrews, although quoting Jeremiah 31:31, expresses the promise as it came directly from God himself. "For finding fault with them, he saith, Behold, the days come, saith the Lord, when I will make a new covenant with the house of Israel and with the house of Judah" (8:8).

Many prophets were sent to Israel and Judah denouncing their sins, pronouncing judgment, and calling for repentance. One obvious and outstanding theme of the prophets' messages was a call to loyalty; a call to return to the covenant relationship they had made with God. But Israel failed. Consequently God mercifully promised to make a new and better covenant with them.

It Was a Different Covenant

Earlier in the ministry of Jeremiah God used him to

give a final call to Judah and Jerusalem to obey the covenant God had given them when He brought them out of Egypt (Jeremiah 11:3-7). Then God proclaimed that both the Northern and Southern Kingdoms had by idolatry broken His covenant and nothing remained for them but judgment (Jeremiah 11:9-12). But even in this darkest hour God gave them a ray of light. Some would return from the captivity. More important, He would make a new and different covenant with them.

How easily and justifiably God could have destroyed Israel. They seemed determined to go their own way and to provoke Him to anger. Truly God's mercy extends far beyond human comprehension. But what about us? Haven't we failed God too? Let's thank Him for the mercy and grace He has extended to us.

Let's look at some of the features of this new covenant. It would involve three major things in particular.

First, there would be a changed heart. Instead of writing His laws and teachings on tables of stone, God would put them in the minds and hearts of His people (verse 10). The Word of God given through Ezekiel is worth repeating: "A new heart also will I give you, and a new spirit will I put within you" (Ezekiel 36:26). When our hearts are cleansed by the blood of Christ, our inclination is to love and serve God.

Second, the knowledge of God would be a matter of personal experience (verse 11). No longer would a human priest be necessary as a mediator. Believers are encouraged to come directly into God's presence.

Third, the sins of all who respond would be blotted out and remembered no more. "As far as the east is from the west, so far hath he removed our transgressions from us" (Psalm 103:12).

81

9

It's All Fulfilled in Christ
Read Hebrews 9:1-28

To gain an appreciation and understanding of the Old Testament with its prophecy, poetry, history, and typology is a most worthy goal. Our lives cannot help but be spiritually enriched as we learn the meanings of the Old Testament types and figures. The apostle Paul tells us that Israel's experiences were written as examples for us (1 Corinthians 10:11), so we could learn by them and not fall into some of the same snares that Israel did.

Unfortunately all Christians have not yet learned the value of understanding Old Testament teaching. This is illustrated by a statement made during a lecture by a well-known and highly respected Bible teacher. At this particular class session his lecture to the students focused on the teachings of Jesus. Knowing his subject very well helped make his classes exciting and interesting. But one statement he made troubled some of the students. "Why should we study the Old Testament," he asked, "when we have the New? Isn't the New Testament a fulfillment of the Old?" he continued.

Hebrews contradicts this point of view. In chapter 9 we shall not only focus on the eternal sacrifice of Christ but also see how beautifully it is prefigured in the Old Testament Scriptures.

The Earthly Sanctuary

How interesting that the writer to the Hebrews should describe in some detail the sanctuary under the old covenant. Hebrews continues to compare the sacrificial ritual under the old covenant with Christ's atoning work. To do this it was necessary to review for the readers the physical arrangement of the wilderness tabernacle and its furnishings. This provided a background for the comparison that is to follow. As we view the tabernacle and its furnishings, notice particularly the temporary nature of it. We should be able to see at once that it wasn't designed with permanency in mind. Even Solomon's and Herod's temples, though more sturdy than the tent in the wilderness, were not intended to be permanent. God had a better plan, a better sacrifice, and a better covenant.

On page 85 is a simple drawing of the tabernacle in the wilderness. It will help us to review the physical arrangement. The first 5 verses of Hebrews 9 give a written description. Read these verses and study the chart carefully. You will be helped greatly in understanding the rest of the chapter.

Functions of the Earthly Priests

Turning from a description of the tabernacle, Hebrews now points to the work of the priests. Every day there were many rituals and tasks that needed to be done. Moses had received from God detailed instructions concerning this work. Each task performed by a priest was considered as service for God (verse 6).

Appointed priests performed services almost continually in the outer court and in the Holy Place. Each day they trimmed the lamps morning and evening (Exodus 27:20, 21). They also burned incense on the golden altar of incense (Exodus 30:7). Then, too, the appointed priests went each week into the Holy Place to put fresh bread on the table of showbread (Leviticus 24:8). Any priest who was duly appointed could perform these services.

Even though the work at times may have seemed commonplace and mundane, the priests daily performed a spiritual service. Their work was ordained and approved by God himself. Yet the priests were limited in the scope of their service. None except the high priest was permitted to enter the second tabernacle or the Holy of Holies. Even then he could enter this holy place only once a year, on the Day of Atonement. Leviticus 16 prescribes the conditions under which he could enter. They were very rigid and had to be carefully kept or death could result.

Why did the high priest go into the Holy of Holies? Or what service did he perform? Again, let's read what the Bible says. "But into the second went the high priest alone once every year, not without blood, which he offered for himself, and for the errors of the people" (Hebrews 9:7). On the Day of Atonement, when the high priest went into the Holy of Holies, he took with him the blood of a bullock and a goat. While there he sprinkled the blood on and before the mercy seat (Leviticus 16:14-16), thus making atonement for his sins and the sins of the people.

Figure of Things to Come

God's provision for the spiritual needs of the Israel-

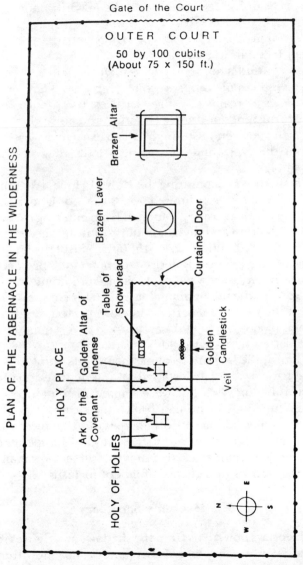

PLAN OF THE TABERNACLE IN THE WILDERNESS

Gate of the Court

OUTER COURT
50 by 100 cubits
(About 75 x 150 ft.)

Brazen Altar

Brazen Laver

Curtained Door

Table of Showbread

Golden Altar of Incense

HOLY PLACE

Golden Candlestick

Ark of the Covenant

Veil

HOLY OF HOLIES

© Copyright 1976 by the Gospel Publishing House, Springfield, Missouri.

N E
W S

ites is beautiful to behold. Yes, the magnificent attire of the priests, the tabernacle with its furnishings, and the system of sacrifices and offerings were designed to help Israel in worshiping God.

Yet, wonderful as it was, the writer tells us these were figures of things to come (verse 9). They were shadows of reality. All the sacrifices, the rituals, and the furnishings prefigured a future and more glorious person and event. Although we can learn many lessons from the types and figures, let's look at several as examples.

First, the veil separating the Holy of Holies from the Holy Place suggests limited access to God. Under the old covenant all were prohibited from entering except the high priest and then he could go only under strictly prescribed conditions. Even though some of the Israelites may have sincerely desired to enter God's presence more freely, they were prohibited from doing so.

Second, the use of animal sacrifices for sin speaks to us of the need for a better and more perfect sacrifice. Their blood couldn't take away sin. It covered sin until the better sacrifice would be made.

Third, the limitations of earthly priests point to the need for a better priesthood. Many of them served faithfully and well but were limited in the scope of their functions by human frailty and death.

All of these along with other types foreshadowed the perfect One who was to come. At God's appointed time, Christ came to earth. Later we will see how many of the figures find their fulfillment in Jesus.

The Heavenly Sanctuary

Hebrews now turns from the shadows and figures so prominent under the old covenant to show how they were fulfilled in Christ. When Jesus appeared, the shadows gave way to the perfect and eternal reality. No longer was there any need for the daily sacrifices or the sin offering. Neither was there any need for earthly priests. Even the tabernacle with all its furnishings and rich typology had served its purpose and had given way to something better.

The writer to the Hebrews directs the attention of the readers away from the earthly sanctuary to the eternal tabernacle. "But Christ being come a high priest of good things to come, by a greater and more perfect tabernacle, not made with hands, that is to say, not of this building" (Hebrews 9:11). How wonderful! Christ our High Priest now ministers in the heavenly sanctuary of which the "tent in the wilderness" was a material copy. Even the glory of Solomon's magnificent temple cannot be compared with the one in the heavens. Praise God! Someday all whose names "are written in the Lamb's book of life" (Revelation 21:27) will learn more about this heavenly sanctuary.

Following His resurrection, Christ ascended into the heavens. He then assumed His high priestly ministry. We are familiar with the functions of the earthly priests under the Levitical system. Their duties were clearly outlined for them. But what are the priestly functions of Christ who has superseded them? Or as He ministers in the heavenly sanctuary, what is the nature of His work? Hebrews gives us a glimpse of Christ ministering in the eternal tabernacle. As we look at the high priestly ministry of Jesus our love and appreciation for Him will grow.

First, He entered the Holy of Holies in the heavenly sanctuary and offered blood as a sacrifice for sin. But it was different from the Levitical atonement. Notice what the Bible says, "Neither by the blood of goats and calves, but by his own blood he entered in once into the holy place, having obtained eternal redemption for us" (Hebrews 9:12). How marvelous and yet how awesome! Christ offered His own blood as the eternal sacrifice for the sins of mankind. Under the old covenant the blood of animals only covered sin. Thank God that was changed by Christ's sacrifice: now our sins are taken away. Unlike the Levitical priests, Christ made the sacrifice only once, but it was complete and eternal.

Second, He became Mediator of the better covenant (verse 15). As we have already seen, a mediator is a go-between. The concept is frequently used in the Old Testament. Moses was a mediator of the old covenant. Sometimes the prophets and kings also served as mediators. Still Christ stands out as the perfect Mediator as He represents God to man and man to God.

Third, Christ intercedes for us before the throne of God (Hebrews 7:25).

Christ's priestly ministry then in the heavenly tabernacle, the one not made with hands, is efficacious and eternal. Never again will an earthly priesthood patterned after that in the Mosaic covenant be needed. Jesus is a priest forever after the order of Melchizedek. Praise God for our eternal compassionate High Priest!

But Death Was Necessary

Understandably, the Hebrew believers received thorough teaching about the old and new covenants. They needed particularly to understand the position of Christ in relationship to both covenants.

As the Holy Spirit guided the writer of Hebrews, he

progressed to yet another truth. In verses 15-22 he declares that death was necessary to bring into effect the provisions of the new covenant or testament. But why in these verses do some translations of the Bible, including the King James, use the word *testament* while others use *covenant*? Is there a difference? Interestingly the New Testament uses one Greek word for testament and covenant. Each is a variant rendering of the same Greek word. Although they are used interchangeably, each contains a shade of meaning different from the other. *Covenant* connotes agreement, while the connotation of *testament* is a last will and testament in which a promised inheritance is involved.

While explaining this aspect of Christ's work, the writer infers the meaning of testament. What he is saying is that the new covenant with its promises of unfettered access to God and eternal salvation must be ratified by death (Hebrews 9:15, 16). Just like a will made out and signed by a person while he is living. The provisions of the will can be claimed and received only after the death of the person or testator.

We see then how the new testament or covenant with all of its promises and provisions was ratified or put into force by the death of Christ. He shed His blood on the cross and made atonement for our sins. Speaking of Christ, the author says: "And for this cause he is the mediator of the new testament, that by means of death, for the redemption of the transgressions that were under the first testament, they which are called might receive the promise of eternal inheritance" (Hebrews 9:15).

Superiority of Christ's Sacrifice

Repeatedly our author exalts Christ and His redemptive work far above all else. Obviously this is a main thrust of Hebrews. Christ is central and is shown to be superior in all phases of His sacrificial and mediatorial work. Understandably, the writer returns to this emphasis again and again. But isn't it a good lesson for us? Shouldn't we, too, exalt Christ above all else? When we invite Him to reign as Lord and master of our lives, God is pleased. Only then can we live a peaceful and fulfilled Christian life. When Christ is not given first place, spiritual conflicts result. Let's determine to let Jesus reign supreme.

To emphasize again the superiority of Christ, the writer gives us another comparison. As the Holy Spirit guides him, he uses comparison and contrast as effective teaching tools.

First, he states that Christ didn't enter a holy place made with hands (verse 24). The implication is that Levitical priests ministered in an earthly tabernacle, but Christ ministers in the sanctuary in heaven itself.

Second, unlike the Levitical high priest who entered the Holy of Holies every year and made the blood atonement, Christ made the sacrifice once (verses 25 and 28). He died once and made atonement for sin. It was eternal.

Christ Will Appear Again

Although the second coming of Christ is a dominant theme in the New Testament, Hebrews says little about it. The writer of Hebrews pictures Jesus as ministering in the heavenly Holy of Holies, but as the Levitical high priest emerged after making the atonement, so will Jesus reappear to those who wait for Him. Notice how the writer puts it. "So Christ was once offered to bear the sins of many; and unto them that look for him shall he appear the second time without sin unto salvation" (Hebrews 9:28). Praise God, He isn't coming to deal with the sin question. That was dealt with decisively at Calvary. When He comes again, all the joys and blessings of our eternal inheritance will be fully realized.

10

A Better Sacrifice
Read Hebrews 10:1-39

Our hearts should rejoice as we meditate on Christ and the glorious work of redemption He accomplished. We stand in awe while contemplating the magnitude of Christ's personal sacrifice. Even though it meant intense suffering and death, His dedication to carry out the divine plan of redemption was complete. There would be no turning back even though His entire being revolted at the thought of becoming sin. Until His sacrifice was complete Jesus would follow the path of obedience, suffering, and humility. He would become the supreme sacrifice for sin. His own blood would be shed for the sins of mankind. In offering His blood, Christ would make the atonement for sin that would do more than cover sins. It would "take away" sin. His sacrifice was perfect and eternal.

Some of the spiritual concepts dealt with in Hebrews 10 have been previously emphasized. They may even seem repetitious. When this occurs, we should keep in mind the intent of the Book of Hebrews: to lead the Jewish believers into a clear understanding of the person and work of Christ. So the author repeatedly emphasizes the superiority of Christ in every aspect of His redemptive work. If we keep this in mind, it will help us to understand why the Holy Spirit guided the author in using some repetition.

A Shadow of Good Things

Under the Law of Moses the animal sacrifice, though prescribed by God, made nothing perfect. Hebrews clearly states this. "For the Law . . . can never with those sacrifices, which they offered year by year continually, make the comers thereunto perfect" (Hebrews 10:1). The sacrifices were not intended by God to make sinners perfect. All the ritual of the Levitical system with the animal sacrifices and peace offerings pointed to the Perfect One who was to come, the One who would "put away" sin and usher in a new era of unhindered fellowship and communion with God. His sacrifice would make possible a relationship between God and man not possible under the Mosaic system.

Continuing to show the imperfections and weaknesses of the Old Testament sacrifices, the author emphasizes another significant point. If the sacrifices prescribed by the Mosaic Law had brought an inner cleansing and purging of sin, there would have been no need to repeat them (verse 2). If the Levitical sacrifices had removed the barriers hindering access to God, they would no longer have been needed.

But they were only shadows of "good things to come" (verse 1). What are the "good things to come" referred to by Hebrews? They embrace the perfect sacrifice of Christ with all that it implies. His high priestly ministry, eternal salvation, and unfettered access to God are included. The old order of sacrifices was imperfect. It could not provide these things.

One point made crystal clear is that it was impossible

for the blood of bulls and goats to take away sin (Hebrews 10:4). All the "good things" made possible by the perfect sacrifice of Christ were not supplied by the old order. How grateful we should be for the cleansing from sin made possible through the precious blood of Christ. Another verse beautifully sums it up for us. "The blood of Jesus Christ his Son cleanseth us from all sin" (1 John 1:7).

What Kind of Offering?

Prophetic utterances referring to the perfect sacrifice of Christ are found throughout the Old Testament. The writer to the Hebrews looks to Psalm 40:6-8 for the appropriate words to describe the appearance of Christ in relation to the sacrifices and offerings. In fact the author, rather than quoting the verses verbatim, paraphrases them.

Before considering this passage, let's review the types of offerings prescribed by the Mosaic Law. Although we use them interchangeably, the terms *offering* and *sacrifice* have both a general and specific designation.

1. *Sacrifice*—Although it can refer to any animal sacrifice, the Old Testament uses it mainly in relation to peace offerings.
2. *Offering*—This also is used in a general way, but in the Levitical system it refers to the sin offering, and meal offering.

Centuries before Christ the Psalmist prophetically declared the Levitical order of offerings and sacrifices as ineffective. They were ineffective because they couldn't change the inner life of a person nor could they provide unhindered access to God. Notice his statement: "Sacrifice and offering thou wouldest not" (Hebrews 10:5).

Not only were the Old Testament sacrifices incomplete, ineffective, and shadowy representations of good things to come, God himself really didn't want them (verse 6). This must have come as a shock to some of the Hebrew Christians. They had been brought up to believe in the superiority of the Levitical sacrifices to those of the heathen that surrounded them. So it must have been difficult for them to believe that God didn't really desire the sacrifices. These sacrifices actually reminded the Israelites of their sins (verse 3), but in contrast, Christ's perfect sacrifice removed all guilt and purged our conscience.

Psalm 40 then is quoted by the writer to contrast the superiority of Christ to the Levitical offerings. They are put in contrast to the body or person of Christ through whom God's will would actually be done. What God desired wasn't sacrifices but to see His will done. It would take a fully obedient person to fulfill it. Christ alone met these requirements.

Following the quotation of Psalm 40:6-8 the author, guided by the Holy Spirit, clinches his point. He presents Christ as the perfect offering. The old order of sacrifices was cancelled and a new one established which centered in the person and work of Christ. In referring to this the author declares: "By the which will we are sanctified through the offering of the body of Jesus Christ once for all" (Hebrews 10:10). What a glorious yet solemn declaration. When thinking of the price that the Saviour paid for our redemption we cannot help but stand in awe. Yet our hearts rejoice while meditating on the complete salvation Christ provided for us.

Most of the Hebrew Christians continued to offer

the old sacrifices even though they had been converted to Christ. Now was the time for them to realize once and for all the old order was gone. It was a waste of time to make the old sacrifices. God isn't pleased by religious ritualism. He desires worship that comes from the heart and from a life that's obedient to His will.

The Eternal Perfect Sacrifice

Calvary forever changed it all. Jesus offered himself as the supreme and perfect sacrifice. His death upon the cross brought eternal salvation to all who believe. As our High Priest, He presented in the heavenly sanctuary His own blood as an atonement for sin. Christ's sacrifice then is a better sacrifice because it met all of God's requirements. It is eternally effective. Hebrews declares that by the one offering Christ forever made perfect in the sight of God those who are sanctified or those who believe in Him (verse 14).

The writer also declares that the Holy Spirit witnesses to us about the effectiveness of Christ's sacrifice and of the new covenant (verse 15). How does the Spirit witness to us? Or what means does He use to communicate the message to us?

First, the Holy Spirit speaks to us through the Word of God. Besides the New Testament passages (as in Hebrews) there are many prophetic utterances in the Old Testament. Jeremiah 31:31-34, along with several passages in the Psalms, are good examples. The revelation of God's Word always builds on what has been previously given. Let's listen to God's Word. As we listen, the Holy Spirit will teach us many wonderful truths.

Second, under the new covenant God has planted

His laws in our hearts. Quoting Jeremiah again, the writer declares: "This is the covenant that I will make with them after those days, saith the Lord; I will put my laws into their hearts, and in their minds will I write them" (Hebrews 10:16 quoted from Jeremiah 31:33). He would also inspire the will and give the power to put those laws or teachings into effect in our lives. Praise God! No longer would there be a mere outward keeping of forms of the old ritualistic system. The absolute forgiveness provided at Calvary through the blood of Christ leaves no room for further sacrifices or sin offerings.

It's the Believer's Privilege

What a difference the new covenant makes. Access to the Holy of Holies under the Law was restricted to the high priest once a year. Unless the Israelites followed the detailed instructions, any violation could result in death. *Now Death is result of those who try to stand before God c/o Christ's covering.*

Again the redemptive work of God's Son changed it all. His sacrifice was perfect. His blood was efficacious. Now every believer comes in prayer not only to heaven's gate but to heaven's inner sanctuary. Yes, into the very presence of God. We are encouraged to come without restrictions and with joy and confidence. In verse 19 the word *boldness* means "joyful confidence" and "perfect freedom." Hebrews expresses this truth beautifully in verse 22: "Let us draw near with a true heart in full assurance of faith."

Some Christians find it difficult to approach God with joy and confidence. They feel that God is so powerful and awesome He should be feared. And in one sense we should fear God. Yet we are encouraged to come right into God's presence with joy and confidence and freedom. Does this imply disrespect? Or irreverence? Or an unwarranted degree of self-confidence? No, definitely not. If our hearts have been cleansed by the blood of Christ, it pleases our Heavenly Father when we manifest a joyful and respectful confidence in Him. So, let's be obedient. Let's respond to God's invitation. He will be pleased and the rewards we receive will be many.

Encouragement to Hold Fast

"Let us hold fast the profession of our faith without wavering; for he is faithful that promised" (Hebrews 10:23). The Hebrew believers needed this charge. How were they going to respond to this advanced instruction? Would they obey it and become mature and strong in the faith? Or would they drift back into the old familiar customs and traditions? The charge to them is to hold fast to the faith.

Could it be that this instruction is just as needed and appropriate for us today? Satan would like for us to drift, to shift our priorities so Christ is not first. If this occurs, our faith is weakened and the danger of our drifting away from Christ is very real.

Take courage, we have a High Priest who caused the veil to be rent. Let's commune and fellowship with God regularly. Let's encourage one another in the faith and provoke one another to love and good works (verse 24). Because some of the Hebrew Christians had neglected corporate worship (verse 25) they are instructed to be more faithful. Attending the house of God regularly is important and necessary. To isolate oneself from the fellowship of believers is a most serious matter. Each believer contributes and receives in public worship. Belonging to a local church and supporting its ministry in the community pleases God. Let's make it a regular habit to worship and fellowship together.

Another Serious Warning

Living up to the knowledge given us by the Holy Spirit is a serious concern. Along with the promises of blessing the Bible also issues many warnings. Like blessings, they too are given for our good.

Verses 26-31 contain a similar warning to that given in chapter 6. Here Hebrews warns that those who slip away and fall back into sin will receive greater judgment than those who despised and disregarded Moses' law (verses 28, 29). The warning is most serious.

Does this passage mean that a Christian who sins cannot repent? Unfortunately many Christians who have made mistakes have despaired by misinterpreting Hebrews 10:26-31. Praise be to God, the way is still open to all who will confess their sins (1 John 1:9; 2:1). The blood of Christ still has its cleansing power. If you have sinned or committed offenses against someone, you should confess, repent, and accept God's forgiveness.

Nevertheless, God's provision of mercy and forgiveness does not minimize the warning Hebrews gives. Some of the Hebrew Christians were in danger of drifting back into a meaningless ritual and finding no forgiveness in the Levitical sacrifices. We too need to take heed. Those who once knew Christ but have turned their backs on Him have nothing to look forward to except eternal judgment. There is no hope for anyone who despises the precious blood of Christ that was shed for the sins of mankind. Indeed, "It is a fearful thing to fall into the hands of the living God" (verse 31).

Call to Steadfastness

Appropriately following this warning, the writer calls for more steadfastness. He issues words of reassurance and encouragement. He reminds them of past trials and how they endured them with confidence. Although the Hebrew believers were in need of teaching, they had been faithful to God. In light of this the writer admonishes them, "Cast not away therefore your confidence, which hath great recompense of reward" (verse 35).

Finally, the writer encourages these believers with the glorious fact of Christ's coming. What a hope this is! What a comfort in time of trial! The Hebrew believers like many today must have been encouraged by this reminder that Jesus is coming again. When you are discouraged or when life is tough, you can rejoice at the hope of Christ's coming. As believers did in other generations, we too look forward to this most glorious event.

11
God's Hall of Fame
Read Hebrews 11:1-40

For those who enjoy sports, Cooperstown should have a special significance. It is a relatively small resort town in eastern New York State, nestled in a very historic setting. Being situated at the south end of Lake Otsego locates it where the Susquehanna River has its origin. It is a community rich in history.

But what makes Cooperstown something special? Among several things, it is the hometown of Abner Doubleday who is credited by some with having invented the game of baseball. An exhibition game is played there each year by representatives of the National and American league professional baseball clubs. Located there, too, is a nationally famous museum. It is called the National Baseball Museum and Hall of Fame and was established in 1939. Walking through the Museum and Hall of Fame, one can see mementos of famous baseball players. It offers an exciting experience for those who enjoy the game of baseball.

God's Word too has a "hall of fame." Our hearts are thrilled as we read the accounts in Hebrews 11 of men and women who defied circumstances and believed God for a miraculous intervention. These spiritual giants stand out in history because of the quality of their faith. They persevered and endured under unbelievably trying conditions. They were men and women, just as we are, who were challenged by an ungodly society and remained faithful to God.

Faith Described

Without doubt the most appropriate way to begin a lesson on faith is to consider the Bible definition. Here it is. "Now faith is the substance of things hoped for, the evidence of things not seen" (Hebrews 11:1).

Let's prayerfully study this definition. First, faith is the substance of things hoped for. Or we could say it is the confident assurance of things hoped for. But what are the things for which one hopes? Perhaps a broader meaning is implied, but to the Old Testament saints it included the promises that God made to them. All the promises of God were so firmly and completely believed that these giants in the faith conducted their daily lives in light of them. Many lived in deprivation but obeyed God because they believed in His promises.

God hasn't changed! We, too, have His promises to meet our every need, to bless us, and to send Christ back and take us to our eternal home (John 14:1-3). Do you really believe God will fulfill His promises? Even here God reminds us of His faithfulness to keep His Word (2 Peter 3:9). Faith, then, is the "eye of the soul" by which we apprehend the reality of the spiritual realm. The natural eye cannot see God, heaven, or the Holy Spirit. Yet we experience their reality when we exercise faith and trust.

Second, faith is the evidence or inner conviction of things not seen. There are many things we have not yet seen. The second coming of Christ, the reality of

102

heaven, and the reign of Christ on earth are only some. Yet we live in constant and joyful expectation of the events. In the natural world "seeing is believing," but in the spiritual world faith reverses the order to "believing is seeing."

Faith Demonstrated

Evidences of faith can be clearly seen in the lives of those who follow and obey God. One of the first members of the human family to demonstrate an unwavering faith was Abel. When he made a sacrifice, God showed His approval by accepting it. This bore witness to the fact that Abel was a righteous man (verse 4).

Let's look at the facts of this account. According to the narrative in Genesis 4:3-15 both brothers brought their offerings to God. Cain, the older brother, brought his offering which consisted of the "fruit of the ground." Being an agriculturalist he brought what was most readily available. Abel, on the other hand, being a shepherd brought the "firstlings of his flock." Both brought offerings, yet God accepted Abel's but rejected Cain's. Why? Much has been written and taught about why one was accepted and the other not.

Some Bible teachers believe Cain's offering was rejected because it wasn't a blood sacrifice. This may be true, although the Genesis account doesn't specifically say it. One thing we are sure of is the significance of one's attitude in worshiping God. Cain was told by God that if he did well he would be accepted, and if he didn't, sin was lying at the door (Genesis 4:7).

Abel by faith brought an offering that pleased God. The Bible teaches that God rejected even a blood sacrifice if it wasn't accompanied by obedience (1 Samuel

15:22). Abel had what Cain lacked, a living faith in God.

Another example of one to whom God bore witness is Enoch. But what gave witness that Enoch pleased God? We are told he walked with God. This in the Old Testament meant a life of humility and obedience—a life, too, that expressed love toward God and love, justice, and mercy toward man (Isaiah 58:10, 11; Micah 6:8). What a testimony! Enoch surely belongs in the spiritual hall of fame. The record states that he walked with God and by faith was translated that he should not see death (verse 5).

Can't Please God Without Faith

To please God one must have faith; so states the Bible. Speaking of this Hebrews declares: "But without faith it is impossible to please him: for he that cometh to God must believe that he is, and that he is a rewarder of them that diligently seek him" (Hebrews 11:6). Apart from faith in God no one can please Him. Even to come to God we must believe that He exists and will reward those who seek Him.

Yet faith that pleases God has certain qualities. Belief in God as the supreme creator and ruler of the universe is a must. Belief, too, in all God's promises, even though some are yet unfulfilled, is essential. He wants us to have complete confidence in Him as the Supreme Being and in the promises He has made. Anything short of this would be insulting to Him.

Anyone who has experienced the love of God through Christ the Saviour should have little difficulty in building a strong faith. Being saved through faith in Christ and having been filled with the precious Holy Spirit, our faith should soar. We have personally witnessed God's faithfulness again and again. How can we help but have faith in Him! Let's please God by believing.

Faith and Obedience

Faith and obedience are complementary. They go hand in hand. Usually where one sees a strong faith in God, a further look will reveal a heart that's inclined toward obedience.

Noah is a good example of how faith and obedience are related. Listen to the Word: "By faith Noah, being warned of God of things not seen as yet, moved with fear, prepared an ark to the saving of his house" (Hebrews 11:7). How did Noah show his faith? And how did it relate to his acting in obedience to God? First, he believed what God told him. His faith didn't waver even though what God warned him about didn't seem possible. Noah and his family lived far from any large body of water, and there was no sign of a flood; yet he believed God. His faith in God's word was unshakable.

Second, his sterling faith in God's word, coupled with a godly fear, motivated him to obey God's direction and build an ark. Was Noah afraid of the Flood? Is that why he built the ark? He may have been afraid of the Flood, but that wasn't why he obeyed God. Then what was it? His reverence toward God made him honor God's word and respect His warnings. Thus Noah quickly obeyed and built the ark.

Abraham is another prime example of how faith and obedience complement each other. His faith was characterized by complete confidence in what God said. When God spoke, Abraham believed and obeyed (verse 8). His faith was expressed in complete obedience. Abraham saw God as a wonderful Friend who loved and cared, so he was willing to commit his life into God's hands. His trust in God was so full and complete that he left his home country at God's command not knowing where he was being led.

Were Abraham's trials over when he reached the Promised Land? Actually they were just beginning. On his arrival he found the land in possession of the Canaanites. Throughout the rest of his life he lived in the Promised Land as an alien. The only part of the land he owned was a burying ground.

But Abraham had faith and a heart inclined to obey. By faith he caught a glimpse of a better country, a heavenly country that was his real home. "For he looked for a city which hath foundations, whose builder and maker is God" (Hebrews 11:10).

They Died in Faith

Referring to those already mentioned, the writer declares, "These all died in faith, not having received the promises, but having seen them afar off" (Hebrews 11:13).

Abraham, Sarah, Isaac, Jacob, and Joseph all received God's promises. They lived in faith. Their lives were characterized by a strong conviction that God would keep His promises. Even in death they continued to believe that God would fulfill His word. Just prior to death both Isaac and Jacob blessed their sons and indicated they still were trusting God (verses 20, 21).

An outstanding characteristic of these godly patriarchs was their attitude toward their homeland. Although they valued an earthly home, they considered themselves to be strangers and pilgrims (Genesis 23:4;

47:9). Their permanent home was no place on this earth. Their faith had caught a vision, or a glimpse of a better country—one with a city prepared for them by God (verse 16).

We too are pilgrims. As beautiful and wonderful as our earthly homes may be, they are temporary at best. Didn't our Lord promise us a new and eternal home, one prepared for us by Christ himself (John 14:1-3)? Our faith doesn't rest in the transient order of things on earth, but in God's eternal promises.

Isaac Offered by Faith

Recorded in verses 17-19 is one of the most remarkable illustrations of complete faith and trust. Abraham had received God's promises, one of them being that he would have numerous posterity even though Sarah was well beyond the normal childbearing years. How their hearts must have rejoiced when Isaac was born. God had kept His promise even when it took a miraculous intervention.

Genesis 22:1-14 records for us the instructions God gave Abraham about offering Isaac as a sacrifice. The death of Isaac could signal the end of God's promise. All hope could die with him. This all could happen, but Abraham's faith told him it wouldn't. His faith assured him that God could provide a lamb for the sacrifice (Genesis 22:8) or if Isaac was actually offered God could raise him from the dead (Hebrews 11:19). Abraham in faith took Isaac to the appointed place for the sacrifice, but he fully expected to bring him back home. Little wonder then the Scriptures declare, "Abraham believed God, and it was accounted to him for righteousness" (Galatians 3:6).

Moses Had Faith Too

Moses had all the privileges and advantages that any young man could ask for in life. He grew up as a prince in Egypt, then the most powerful nation on earth. Pharaoh's daughter considered Moses to be her favorite son. Undoubtedly he was trained in the best schools of his time. What young man in any generation wouldn't have been proud and satisfied with the advantages afforded him. He could have looked forward to a life of honor and prosperity.

Yet the Bible declares that he turned his back on all these privileges and chose to suffer affliction with the people of God (Hebrews 11:24, 25). But why? Because he believed God and His promises. Then, too, he saw Israel, not as helpless slaves, but as the people of God. They were destined to become the light of the nations; destined to prepare the way for the Messiah. By faith too he accepted the promises made to Abraham that God would bless all the families of the earth through his descendants. So Moses accepted the challenge. True, he needed training and experience before God could use him, but it all started with faith in God's promises. All that Moses accomplished was through faith. Forsaking Egypt (verse 27), crossing the Red Sea (verse 29), and leading Israel through the wilderness required faith.

After Moses died, Joshua by faith led Israel against Jericho. Rahab, too, was spared because she believed. The Old Testament is filled with accounts of men and women who conquered the enemy through faith.

Faith's Trials and Assurances

A common error among many Christians is to believe that the closer one lives to God the fewer trials will be encountered. Some very sincere believers have been greatly disillusioned by clinging to this mistaken and unbiblical notion. True followers of God in every generation of time have been tried and tested, sometimes severely, even unto death.

Let's look to the Word of God to shed more light on this subject so we can understand it better and conduct our lives accordingly.

None of the hall of famers or spiritual giants mentioned in Hebrews 11 lived their lives without encountering severe trials and testings. Although they followed God loyally and faithfully, testings came that sometimes involved great suffering. The Holy Spirit through the author gives a description of some things suffered by the men and women of God. Hebrews 11:35-37 lists some for us: imprisonments, torture, mockings, scourgings, stonings, death by the sword, wanderings in the desert, and being destitute and even tormented.

But why is it that God's people in every generation have been severely tested? Although we don't understand the "whys" in full, it is true that trials help us to grow in the Lord. Again the Bible will help us gain an understanding: "The trial of your faith, being much more precious than of gold that perisheth" (1 Peter 1:7). Although God doesn't want to see His children suffer, sometimes it is necessary to help us learn lessons and grow in Him.

But Praise God, even through the most severe trials or testings we can have complete assurance that God is in control. We may not understand why, but inherent in our definition of faith is the evidence or "complete assurance" that God will keep His promises to us. God has never failed. Let's believe Him and cling to His promises.

12
Running the Race
Read Hebrews 12:1-29

As Kevin walked in the door that warm spring afternoon he called to his mother. He usually came home from school bubbling with ideas and was always ready to talk about them with anyone who would listen. But this was a special day. After going from room to room looking for his mother and not finding her, Kevin hurried out through the patio doors into the backyard. There was Mother manicuring a newly planted flower garden.

"Mom," Kevin exclaimed, "I signed up for the high school track team today. Is it all right?"

"Great," answered his mother. "But are you certain you want to spend the time and effort it takes to train? Mr. Barclay, the track coach, called today and said how delighted he was that you joined the team. But he also said it would be necessary for you to come to school early every morning to train and practice running."

"I know the training is difficult, Mom," Kevin said, "but it's worth it."

In the Bible the Christian life is sometimes compared to an athletic contest. The salvation experience brings with it great joy and peace, but it also brings conflict. As the athlete deprives himself of many tem-

110

porary comforts and pleasures to win a crown, so must the Christian learn self-discipline. God's Word instructs and encourages the believer to grow in the grace and knowledge of God (2 Peter 3:18). Recorded too in Hebrews 12 are strong words of encouragement for Christians to strive for spiritual growth and maturity—to go beyond the rudiments of salvation (Hebrews 6:1) and to develop into mature believers.

Let's Run the Race

Most people seek a way of life that brings a high degree of satisfaction. There is something within all of us that seeks and enjoys a challenge. It may be to climb a mountain, swim the English channel, or redecorate a room exercising one's artistic skill. Children and young people, too, enjoy a challenge. Many school and community activities are designed to be an outlet for this urge.

Perhaps this is one reason why the challenge to live a Christian life appeals to so many people everywhere. It's not surprising then when the Bible likens the Christian life to an athletic contest. Listen to Hebrews: "Let us lay aside every weight, and the sin which doth so easily beset us, and let us run with patience the race that is set before us" (Hebrews 12:1). How interesting. But this isn't the first time the Bible compares the Christian life to a race or athletic contest. The apostle Paul likened it to a race in 1 Corinthians 9:24 and Galatians 5:7.

But what are the similarities between an athletic contest and the Christian life? Or how can we compare them? First, an athlete must follow strict training rules if he is to compete successfully in a sports event. Train-

111

ing isn't easy. Many rise early in the morning to run several miles. This activity is followed by other forms of strenuous exercise. Then too only certain foods are eaten to assure proper weight control.

As Christians we too must lay aside every weight that might impede our progress. Sins, bad habits, excesses in any area of life, and anything that contributes to pride or self-righteousness must go. For the Hebrew Christian this meant laying aside the old Jewish traditions and ritualism. In our lives it can be anything the Holy Spirit reveals as a hindrance to our spiritual progress.

We read in the Scriptures how the great Christian heroes ran the race. The heroes of Hebrews 11 surround us with evidence that the race of life can be run successfully and victoriously, even under adverse conditions. This great cloud of witnesses (verse 1) gives us a glowing example of faith, vision, patience, and obedience. When we are tempted to give up, let's take courage from the fact that multitudes before us ran the race and gained the prize—eternal life.

Second, in an athletic contest a prize awaits the winner. Even though in New Testament times the prize was only a wreath of leaves that soon wilted in the hot sun, it was considered well worth the effort. To win was most important. Winning the prize erased from the athlete's mind the toils of training.

Praise God, a prize awaits every Christian who runs the race of life successfully. Unlike most earthly contests we can all be winners. Again notice what the Bible says: "And when the chief Shepherd shall appear, ye shall receive a crown of glory that fadeth not away" (1 Peter 5:4).

Looking Unto Jesus

Although this great cloud of witnesses, these heroes of the faith, are an inspiration to us, we need to look beyond them to Jesus. They are good examples for us, but in the race of life we need more than examples. In the Christian race there is a conflict, a very real battle. The apostle Paul tells us our fight is not against flesh and blood but against evil and satanic powers (Ephesians 6:12). Wicked and demonic forces are set against us and would destroy us if it weren't for the power of Christ in our lives. Our faith is challenged daily by these evil powers. We can readily understand then why the Holy Spirit encourages and instructs us in this manner. "Looking unto Jesus the author and finisher of our faith" (Hebrews 12:2). Only as we look to Jesus do we find both the example and help we really need.

Jesus is our example. He is our help. There is no enemy too great for Him. In fact Jesus has already conquered every enemy, every evil power. Having already reached the goal, He can offer us help and He knows how to lead us and to perfect our faith. Then we too can reach the goal.

Those who look to Jesus will understand too that there is only one way. There are no shortcuts, no easy paths to victory. Believing on Jesus (Acts 16:31) and taking up our cross and following Him (Matthew 16:24) will lead us to victory. Looking to Jesus, trusting Him, and relying on Him for spiritual strength are the keys that unlock the door to a victorious and joyful Christian life.

Chastening—Needful but Not Pleasant

Chastening is a term used quite frequently in the

Scriptures in its various forms. Before considering the word as it is used in Hebrews 12, let's define it in clearly understandable terms. Chasten simply means discipline. Sometimes it implies correction or even punishment. Chastening also implies unpleasant treatment which is intended to bring correction, teach discipline, or even to punish for wrong behavior.

The author begins by reminding the Hebrew Christians of the sufferings Christ endured. Although we may never fully comprehend or understand what Christ suffered, it is good for us to recount it often. When we consider our sufferings in contrast to His, it will help us to run the race with endurance even under trying circumstances. Although some Christians had undoubtedly been martyred by this time, the Hebrew believers are reminded that as yet they hadn't resisted unto blood (verse 4). Perhaps the Holy Spirit was preparing them for what was to come.

Although there are many lessons we can learn about chastening, there are five that every believer should know and clearly understand. Let's review them in light of Hebrews 12:4-11.

First, be assured if you are a child of God that chastening will come. We can say without fear of contradiction that every true follower of God in every generation needs to learn discipline. But why? Weren't the heroes of chapter 11 great saints of God? Yes they were. But they became giants of the faith through discipline taught by God (Hebrews 11:35-40). Are Christians today exceptions? No. We too must expect chastening. Whether we are strong or weak, mature or immature, God has lessons for us to learn.

Second, God is the one who chastens us. We can't blame it on Satan or people. It is one of God's finest teaching tools. In teaching us discipline He may use people or circumstances or even deprivation. Nevertheless chastening even though unpleasant is motivated by love. Listen: "For whom the Lord loveth he chasteneth, and scourgeth every son whom he receiveth" (Hebrews 12:6).

Third, we are admonished not to despise chastening (verse 5). It is unfortunate that many Christians today rebel at the slightest deprivation or discomfort. God doesn't want us to be so tied to the comforts of life that any loss of them brings undue sorrow or disappointment. Our joy and happiness should come from our relationship with Christ and not from things or pleasant conditions.

Fourth, we acknowledge, as does the Bible, that any chastening is not pleasant (verse 11). Learning discipline in any area of life isn't always a joyous experience. The athlete in training works hard. He gives up many pleasures commonly enjoyed by other people. Christians, too, recognize that chastening sometimes hurts—it's unpleasant—but we shouldn't despise it. We have learned that our God does all things well. He is our Heavenly Father and He always knows what is best.

Fifth, chastening, though unpleasant, is designed by God for our good (verse 10). It corrects weaknesses and teaches us to live disciplined lives. All this is done for our spiritual growth and development. It is only as we learn to live disciplined lives that God is glorified. So let's thank God for His chastening; it demonstrates the great love our Heavenly Father has for us.

Make Straight Paths

Upon concluding the instruction about chastening, the writer returns to the athletic figure of speech.

115

"Wherefore lift up the hands which hang down, and the feeble knees; and make straight paths for your feet" (Hebrews 12:12, 13). Some of the Hebrew believers had become weary and faint in their minds and souls. The pressures and difficulties of the race were taking their toll. Like cross-country runners in a race that seems too long, their arms were drooping and their knees were ready to buckle. By faith we can straighten up and claim the strength and healing of body, mind, and soul that will enable us to continue in the race.

"Make straight paths for your feet," instructs the Holy Spirit, "lest that which is lame be turned out of the way; but let it rather be healed" (verse 13). But what does this mean? And to whom is the teaching directed?

To make straight paths is a figure of speech. It is saying to the Hebrew Christians: "Be a good example to those who will follow you and to the weak in the faith by leaving the Levitical system behind. Let your faith rest in Christ alone. Look unto Him. As your Saviour and High Priest, He is all you need. Now is the time to make a clean break with the Levitical order of sacrifices. The priesthood too has been superseded by Christ." By taking this action they would become good examples to all who would follow and to those who were still clinging to Judaism.

Do you suppose this instruction has an application for Christians in our time? Yes it does. Are we not also instructed by the Word to be examples? to be witnesses for Christ? Let us accept this challenge and lay aside every weight and sin that weakens our spiritual lives and our testimony. As we avoid getting entangled with the cares of this life, God will be able to use us more effectively in His work here on earth.

Follow Peace with All Men

Quiet and peaceful living is something to be desired. Although we live in a turbulent world characterized by social and political upheaval we should strive for peace. A Christian should take active steps to create peaceful and harmonious relationships. If discord and strife exist, let it not be said that one who loves Christ has fostered them. The Bible is abundantly clear in its instructions to us: "Follow peace with all men" (Hebrews 12:14); and, "Blessed are the peacemakers" (Matthew 5:9). Christians who live peaceful lives and are emissaries of God's peace are called blessed or spiritually happy. How different from the person who fosters strife and dissension. There is usually an atmosphere of gloom about him.

To live peacefully one must diligently cultivate an intimate relationship with God; a relationship that is strong and maintained daily. When we are spiritually strong, we can guard against a "root of bitterness" springing up in us (verse 15), or falling into immorality (verse 16), or selling our spiritual birthright as did Esau (verse 16).

The Superiority of the New Covenant

Again Hebrews uses the element of contrast as a most effective teaching tool. Without mentioning the term *old covenant,* the writer contrasts its weaknesses and imperfections with the new covenant. He points out some differences between the giving of the Law and the receiving of the new covenant or gospel.

The author describes the awesome and fear-provoking circumstances that surrounded the giving of the Law at Sinai. Smoke engulfed the mountain and ascended upward. The mountain shook and God descended on it in fire. The Israelites were terror-stricken as Moses spoke to God. Even a beast that touched Mount Sinai had to be killed. The description found in Hebrews 12:18-21 is based on the account recorded in Exodus 19 and 20.

But, says the author, you have come to the city of the living God (verse 22). You have become a member of the church of the firstborn and your name is written in heaven (verse 23). And further, you have come to Jesus the mediator of the new covenant who offered His own blood in the heavenly Holy of Holies.

Listening and Obeying Are a Must

Again and again the Holy Spirit through the Word issues a serious warning. The last few verses of chapter 12 warn again about listening to God and obeying Him. Those who fail to take heed will not escape God's judgment. Being a Christian is indeed a privilege, but it also carries with it some awesome responsibilities. The writer declares that if people under the old and imperfect covenant received judgment for not hearing and obeying, how can we expect to escape (verse 25). Yet fear beyond a godly fear shouldn't cloud our lives. Hebrews sums it up beautifully for us, "Let us have grace, whereby we may serve God acceptably with reverence and godly fear" (Hebrews 12:28).

13

Practical
Christian Living
Read Hebrews 13:1-25

They had just completed the study of Hebrews up through chapter 12. Only chapter 13 remained. The students had greatly enjoyed studying the Book of Hebrews. Minutes before the class was to end, a young lady raised her hand in a gesture that indicated she wanted to ask a question. Upon being recognized by the teacher she commented, "What we have learned from Hebrews has greatly enriched our spiritual lives. It has helped us to gain many insights about the new covenant." Then came the question: "Does Hebrews also give instruction on practical Christian living like some of the other Epistles?" she asked.

Yes, there is another side to Hebrews—a highly practical side. Contained in chapter 13 is a wealth of practical instruction on everyday Christian living. We must remember that true Christianity is also a very down-to-earth religion. While living a spiritual life, the Christian at the same time must maintain a right relationship to his family, his community, and the world. Hebrews then, besides dealing with a variety of theological topics, also gives teaching in practical Christian living. The Holy Spirit knew the needs, temptations, and problems all believers would face.

Let's accept the challenges presented in chapter 13. We should prayerfully ask God for the will and power to incorporate these teachings into our manner of living.

Responsible in Relationships

Enjoying the rich spiritual blessings that God so graciously sends is a privilege of every Christian. Our lives are greatly enriched as we sit in God's presence and enjoy communion with Him.

Yet we all must come down from the clouds and interact with many other people in our daily living. Every Christian is constantly involved in a network of relationships with others from different walks of life. The last chapter of Hebrews gives some solid advice on how a believer should conduct himself in these relationships. While we consider this instruction as it relates to the Hebrew Christians, let's remember it also has an application for us today.

First, we should let love be the motivating force in every relationship. Hebrews makes it imperative. Notice the words: "Let brotherly love continue" (Hebrews 13:1). Our hearts should be tender toward others. Yes, both to Christians and to those who aren't believers. Admittedly it is not always the easiest way. Yet the expression of brotherly love by Christians in the Early Church went far beyond a feeling of good will. It often was very costly. They shared what they had. They didn't put any limits on their love even to the risking of their lives (James 2:8; 1 John 3:16-18). If we ask God, He will help us to develop this kind of love. Christ is honored when our love reaches out to all kinds of people.

Second, we should practice hospitality. But what

does hospitality mean? Should it also include those who are outside of our circle of friends? Yes. Hospitality simply means that we take the initiative to invite others to share what we have. When we are motivated by love, we reach far beyond our close circle of friends to everyone, including strangers (verse 2). In Bible times desert people especially practiced a well-defined code of hospitality. The ancient law of the desert required that hospitality be extended to those who sought it. Abraham, for example, observed it (Genesis 18:2-5).

Even today, although conditions are different, more than one church has experienced revival when Christians began opening their homes to friends and neighbors.

Third, we should remember our fellow Christians who are going through suffering and trials (verse 3). Specifically mentioned are those in prison for the Lord's sake and those suffering persecution. But we may not have these same conditions today, at least not in our part of the world. How then can we fulfill this Christian obligation? Can we not extend a helping hand to any Christian who is in need? to those in hospitals or nursing homes? Again love should be the motivating force. When we are filled with the Holy Spirit and with God's love, our desire should be to help a suffering brother. Or to share with him our time and prayers that he might be encouraged and strengthened in the Lord. Let's remember in prayer, too, those in other countries who might even be in prison.

Fourth, we should let love reign in the home and observe high moral standards (verse 4). When the husband-wife relationship is troubled, there is little possibility they will show Christian hospitality, or that they will work together to win strangers to the Lord. Also, if the marriage is troubled, there is little chance that either husband or wife will be able to help suffering Christians. The home is still the fundamental unit of society. A strong positive marriage relationship is essential to a happy and God-honoring Christian home. This home is characterized by peace and contentment. Its members are free to share Christ with others in the community and to help fellow Christians who are suffering or in need.

Wise Instruction

One of the great temptations to those who live in an affluent society is covetousness. The old cliche, "The more you have the more you want," is all too true in many cases. Hebrews issues a clear warning about this. "Let your conversation be without covetousness" (verse 5). The Christian should be free from the love of money and from the greed for earthly possessions (1 Timothy 3:3). Didn't our Lord warn us that life does not consist in the abundance of things we possess (Luke 12:15)? Pursuing the goals of our materialistic society has brought grief and disillusionment to many Christians.

When a Christian is free from greed and the love of money, he is more likely to be contented. Whether we have much or little of this world's goods, we can live a contented Christian life. Neither poverty nor riches should be our goal. Our trust in Christ should be complete. When our dedication to Christ is complete, our condition in life is characterized by peace and contentment. Remember, it was Christ who promised, "I will never leave thee, nor forsake thee" (Hebrews 13:5).

Interestingly, the writer in verse 7 reminds the Hebrew believers to recall the faith of their leaders who perhaps had already gone on to be with the Lord. Their faith was strong and their lives worthy of being an example.

Aren't we also encouraged by the godly example set by Christian leaders who have already gone to be with Jesus? Let's remember a strong Christian testimony doesn't end at death. A godly influence sometimes lives on even for centuries after the person has been called to his heavenly home.

Our Unchangeable Lord

One primary characteristic of human society is change—change in every phase of life. The fields of transportation, communication, medicine, education, and others are constantly changing. Not only are they in the process of change, but they are producing constant change in many other areas of life. Our society then is pulsating with change.

In all the confusion and anxiety that result, individuals are desperately looking for an anchor or a stable mooring. Praise God, as Christians we have an anchor. Listen to what the Word declares: "Jesus Christ the same yesterday, and today, and for ever" (Hebrews 13:8). The trustworthiness of Jesus is fully known by those who love Him. Didn't Jesus always keep His word while He was on earth? Also, wasn't He proven to be completely reliable and dependable? We serve the same Lord. He is our Anchor. When everything else seems to be changing, Christ is the same. Our faith and hope for eternal salvation are firmly anchored in the One who does not change.

Established in Doctrine

From the beginning Christians have been challenged by many and varied false doctrines. Satan has tried in various ways to induce Christians to believe a lie. False teachers have arisen in every generation since the establishing of the Church on earth. In fact, the temptation to believe a lie was first encountered by Adam and Eve in the Garden.

But just how important is doctrine anyway? According to Scripture, doctrine is most important. Our beliefs on a given subject not only color our attitudes but also greatly affect our actions. Actually our beliefs determine the course our lives take.

Knowing and believing what the Bible teaches about any given doctrine is of critical importance to a Christian. Let's look at several short passages from the Bible that clearly indicate what God's attitude toward doctrine is.

"Be not carried about with divers and strange doctrines" (Hebrews 13:9).

"Take heed unto thyself, and unto the doctrine" (1 Timothy 4:16).

"That he may be able by sound doctrine both to exhort and to convince the gainsayers" (Titus 1:9).

In the New Testament alone there are over 35 specific references to doctrine using the word itself. Of course there are numerous references to doctrine when one considers the other words, such as "teachings," that also refer to it.

Remember, the Hebrew believers were being bombarded with conflicting and sometimes strange teachings. To counteract this the Holy Spirit warns them not to be swayed or carried about with divers and strange doctrines.

What about Christians in our day? Is there an application of this warning for us? Yes there is. We are privileged to live in a glorious time, an era when God is fulfilling the prophecy given by His servant Joel. The blessed Holy Spirit is being poured out on all flesh or on people all over the world. Men, women, young people, and those farther along in years are receiving the promise of the Spirit. Praise God! It is wonderful to live in this era even though it may well usher in the last days of time before the coming of the Lord.

Yet amidst this mighty outpouring of the Holy Spirit is a tendency by some to embrace and teach doctrines that have no sound Biblical foundation. Human views interwoven with Scripture passages can be very misleading. So, let's maintain a sound Biblical approach to doctrine.

Sacrifices That Please God

Because there still was too much dependence on the Levitical sacrificial system, Hebrews again points out their uselessness under the new covenant. To illustrate this, the Holy Spirit in verses 10-16 turns our attention back to the sin offering under the old Law. Priests could eat of some sacrifices, but not of the sin offerings (Leviticus 6:30). These had to be burned outside the camp. This points up the fact that priests in Jerusalem who held to their old ceremonies and ate the meat of many sacrifices, couldn't partake of the benefits of Christ's sacrifice or our Christian altar while they continued to do so. Depending on these sacrifices under the new covenant is a waste of time. Even under the Mosaic system the imperfections of the sacrifices limited their effectiveness.

What kind of sacrifice then pleases God? When

125

these Hebrew believers made a complete break with the Levitical order, what sacrifices could they make that would please God? Or what takes the place of the Old Testament sacrifices in the everyday life of the Christian? God's Word again gives us the answer: "By him therefore let us offer the sacrifice of praise to God continually, that is, the fruit of our lips giving thanks to his name" (Hebrews 13:15). Instead of the ritual and pageantry of the Levitical system, our worship is filled with praise. Praise itself is a sacrifice that pleases God.

But this is not entirely new! People even in the Old Testament times knew how to praise God. Listen to one of them. "Because thy loving-kindness is better than life, my lips shall praise thee" (Psalm 63:3). So, why not join with other Christians and lift up your voice in praise to God? When this is done in the name of Jesus, it pleases God.

Final Exhortation

Appropriately the last few verses of Hebrews are a final exhortation about Christian living. When learned and followed, these truths greatly enrich one's life and make him more productive for God. Actually some of the suggestions give other ways that Christians can offer praise to God.

First, we are encouraged to do good and to share our blessings in a spirit of Christian fellowship (verse 16). If we really believe God is with us, supplying our needs, we will happily share both material and spiritual blessings with others. A generous spirit should be a mark of every believer. The love we have in our hearts for God should motivate us to share the rich spiritual blessings with others.

Giving our personal testimony of deliverance from

sin can encourage others to accept Christ. Telling others about our experience of receiving the Holy Spirit can create in them a deep spiritual hunger, a hunger that will refuse to be satisfied until the individual too is filled with the Spirit.

Doing good deeds for others in the name of Christ is a powerful testimony in itself. Besides, we receive a deep satisfaction from being obedient to the Holy Spirit.

Second, we should pray for others (verse 18). In addition to trustful obedience and submission to our leaders, we should pray for them. The writer to the Hebrews requests special prayer so he might be able to come back and minister to them. Let's make it a regular habit to remember in prayer our leaders in the faith. Our pastors along with other leaders in the church need our prayers too.

Third, we need to trust Jesus to make us complete in every good work (verse 21). If we are not careful, our work for God can become mere routine. When this happens, much of our effectiveness is lost. Let's do everything in the name of Jesus.

Finally, all that we do should be well-pleasing in His sight. To glorify and honor Christ our Saviour and eternal High Priest should be our goal. This can become a reality in our lives as we trust and lean on Him.